T0078234

BOOKS CO-AUTHORED BY
DONNA SAMMONS CARPENTER:

The Price Waterhouse Guide to Personal Financial Planning

The Price Waterhouse Guide to the New Tax Law

The Price Waterhouse Personal Tax Advisor

The Price Waterhouse Retirement Planning Advisor

The Fall of the House of Hutton

BRIGHT IDEAS

THE INS AND OUTS OF FINANCING A COLLEGE EDUCATION

DONNA SAMMONS CARPENTER

A FIRESIDE BOOK
PUBLISHED BY SIMON & SCHUSTER
NEW YORK LONDON TORONTO SYDNEY TOKYO SINGAPORE

FIRESIDE
Simon & Schuster Building
Rockefeller Center
1230 Avenue of the Americas
New York, New York 10020

Designed by Black Angus Design Group
Manufactured in the United States of America

10   9   8   7   6   5   4   3   2   1

Library of Congress Cataloging in Publication Data

Carpenter, Donna Sammons.
  Bright ideas : the ins and outs of financing a college education / by
Donna Sammons Carpenter.
       p.   cm.
  "A Fireside book."
  Includes index.
  1. Student aid—United States.   2. College costs—United
States.   3. Parents—United States—Finance, Personal.   4. College
students—United States—Finance, Personal.   5. Investments—United
States.   I. Title.
LB2337.4.C373   1992
378.3'0973—dc20   91-37172
                                                                CIP

ISBN 0-671-66633-9

ACKNOWLEDGMENTS

My thanks to the people at
Wordworks—Abby Solomon and Tom
Richman—to my agent Helen Rees
and my editor Julie Merberg

—Donna Carpenter

Contents

I

LONG BEFORE THE BILLS ARE DUE

CHAPTER 1

QUESTIONS YOU'LL WANT TO ANSWER

Baby Willie can't even talk yet, and you're thinking about how you're going to pay for his college education? Good for you.

Except for a full scholarship to the school of his or her choice, the single biggest aid to any parents financing their child's college education is an early start. Given enough time, almost anything is possible—even meeting skyrocketing private higher education costs.

Something else you gain by starting your planning and saving-for-college program early is flexibility and choice. Wait until Willie is sixteen to start making preparations, and the school he decides he wants to attend may not even be an option. Furthermore, if you have, say, eighteen years to get the money together, you have many more saving and investment options available to you than do parents who wait to plan until college looms just a year or two away.

One other powerful argument for getting started early on a college-saving program is that Willie himself can become a part of it; it's his education, after all. Children who have some appreciation of how much is involved in financing college usually show a great deal more respect for the opportunity, both in the academic preparation for school and while they're there, than kids who have it handed to them. The best way we know to build this appreciation is to get Willie involved at any early stage. His efforts should be part of the planning and of the saving.

You don't have to wait until Willie is old enough to start making decisions about schools and courses of study. *Planning* to pay for college can start any time, and the sooner the better for you both.

In this chapter, we'll help you ask yourself some of the big questions that crop up in families with college-bound children. The answers to these questions will help you make your plans.

• WHAT KIND OF COLLEGE?

Whether Willie attends an expensive private school or goes to State U will make a big difference in the tuition bill.

Until you know what kind of college he will attend, your plans should probably be based on the more expensive alternative. Then if Willie picks the less expensive school (and it picks him), the worst that can happen is that you end up with more money set aside than you need.

• WHO WILL PAY?

Who will be responsible for paying Willie's tuition? What about his room and board? His school fees and pocket money? Parents and their children, of course, should discuss and work out these issues. Grandparents and aunts and uncles, if appropriate, can be brought into the planning, too.

This should be worked out long before Willie has started his freshman year. Early planning avoids later misunderstandings and disappointments.

• CAN YOUR CHILD AFFORD COLLEGE?

The answer is yes—but not unconditionally so. Almost every private college and university today claims that ability to pay isn't a factor in its admission decision. They also say that financial aid is available to students who can't afford the full expense of college.

So why bother to save if the school is going to help? Well, if you're very wealthy now and expect to be wealthy when Willie starts school, then you *don't* have to worry about saving or about financial aid. You can just pay the bills out of your income or trust fund or wherever you get your money.

On the other hand, if you're very poor, and can't save, you also don't have to worry. If an expensive school admits Willie and you and he are destitute, chances are the school will find a way to help you finance it.

The worry comes to the bulk of us who occupy the middle. What the schools and the other sources of financial aid that we'll cover in the chapters that follow won't forgive or overlook is our failure to make plans ourselves. They may, for instance, offer loans to the ill-prepared, but the burden of the resulting debt may be more than you want to take on. Effectively, then, middle-class kids whose parents have made no provision to cover the cost of college do run the risk of being disappointed. The good news is that, with planning, there is no reason why they have to be.

• HOW DO YOU HELP YOUR CHILD CHOOSE A SCHOOL THAT YOU CAN AFFORD?

In most cases, the way children and their parents go about selecting colleges to which they'll apply is very unscientific. Maybe there's a family tradition of going to a particular school, or there's only one school that offers the unusual course of study that your child feels he or she must have.

But most high school students have far more college opportunities open to them than they could ever evaluate. And, for most students, there are probably many colleges that would meet their needs about equally well. Some will cost more than others without being academically any better. We're not going to tell you how to influence your child's selection of schools to help ensure that he or she won't be disappointed by the family's inability to meet the cost. But here's one idea to bear in mind.

Parents who have already been through the selection and application process have found that, with kids, visual impressions count for a lot. After all the catalogues have been read and all the guidance counselor's advice absorbed, there's still nothing as impressive to most children as seeing a campus.

Finally, it's something tangible, a real focus for their fantasies of what college is going to be like. If you know that you can't swing the cost of a school, try to discourage Willie from paying a visit there. Other more affordable institutions will be just as impressive to a sixteen- or seventeen-year-old.

With these basic questions out of the way, let's take a look at how to estimate the amount you'll need to save.

CHAPTER 2

WHAT'S IT REALLY GOING TO COST?

How much will college cost? The answer depends, naturally, on what type of college education your child wants and where.

When you know these factors, or at least have some ideas about them, you can start estimating their cost. Then you can figure out what sort of a savings and investment program your family will need to cover these expenses.

In this chapter, we'll help you sort through those questions and show you how to start the estimates.

• WHAT WILL COLLEGE COST?

You've made one decision: your child is heading for college. Now you must decide what amount you should squirrel away on a regular basis to meet your anticipated expenses.

To come up with a rough estimate of how much money you'll require, fill out the worksheet below.

You probably shouldn't try to pinpoint the amount more

1. Enter your child's age   2
2. Years to college; time to invest (18 minus your
    child's age)   16
3. Annual college costs
    Enter (a) $12,000 for a public school or
    (b) $20,000 for a private school $ 12,000
4. College inflation factors   2.54
    According to the College Board, college costs are
    increasing at 6 percent per year. Refer to Table 1
    at the end of the chapter for the inflation factor
    based on your time horizon.
5. Future annual cost of college $ 30,480
    Line 3 times line 4
6. Future total cost of college $121,920
    Line 5 times number of years of college, usually 4.

© FMR Corp. 1990

1. Enter your child's age   _____
2. Years to college; time to invest (18 minus your
    child's age)   _____
3. Annual college costs $_____
    Enter (a) $12,000 for a public school or
    (b) $20,000 for a private school
4. College inflation factors   _____
    According to the College Board, college costs are
    increasing at 6 percent per year. Refer to Table 1
    at the end of the chapter for the inflation factor
    based on your time horizon.
5. Future annual cost of college   _____
    Line 3 times line 4
6. Future total cost of college   _____
    Line 5 times number of years of college, usually 4.

© FMR Corp. 1990

accurately at this stage—particularly if your children are quite young. You face far too many unknowable variables—for example, how much your investments will earn, the state of the economy for the next few years, and so on.

What follows is a sample college-funding worksheet with the answers filled in, then a blank worksheet for your own use. (These worksheets were designed by Fidelity Investments, a Boston-based mutual fund company, and are reprinted with its permission.)

• HOW MUCH SHOULD YOU INVEST?

Now that you know how much college is going to cost, you need to establish an investment target. The easiest and least

---

SAMPLE WORKSHEET

6.	Future total cost of college	$121,920
	Line 6 from previous worksheet	
7a.	Lump sum	4.59
	To determine how much you should set aside today to meet future college costs (assuming a 10 percent rate of return), refer to Table 2 at the end of the chapter and enter the applicable return rate factor	
7b.	Lump sum investment required	$ 26,562
	Divide line 6 by line 7a	
8a.	Periodic investments	35.95
	To determine annual, quarterly, or monthly investment targets, refer to Table 3 at the end of the chapter and enter the applicable return rate factor	
8b.	Annual target amount	$ 3,391
	Divide line 6 by line 8a	
8c.	Monthly target amount	$ 283
	Divide line 8b by 12	
8d.	Quarterly target amount	$ 848
	Divide line 8b by 4	

---

6. Future total cost of college   _____
    Line 6 from previous worksheet
7a. Lump sum   _____
    To determine how much you should set aside
    today to meet future college costs (assuming a 10
    percent rate of return), refer to Table 2 at the end
    of the chapter and enter the applicable return
    rate factor
7b. Lump sum investment required   _____
    Divide line 6 by line 7a
8a. Periodic investments   _____
    To determine annual, quarterly, or monthly
    investment targets, refer to Table 3 at the end
    of the chapter and enter the applicable return
    rate factor
8b. Annual target amount   _____
    Divide line 6 by line 8a
8c. Monthly target amount   _____
    Divide line 8b by 12
8d. Quarterly target amount   _____
    Divide line 8b by 4

© FMR Corp. 1990

stressful way to meet your target is to invest faithfully a fixed amount at periodic intervals—annually, quarterly, or monthly —for a specified number of years. To get an estimate of the amount you'll have to put away to meet your goals, fill out the worksheet that follows using the tables we've provided at the end of the chapter.

TABLE 1—COLLEGE INFLATION FACTORS

It's no secret that inflation plays a role when it comes to the amount of money you'll need to cover the cost of college for your child. The College Board reports that the current annual rate at which college costs are rising is 6 percent. To figure out the inflation factor that applies to your child, choose a figure in the left-hand column and match it with the inflation factor to the right. Then, on line 4 of your worksheet, enter that factor.

TABLE 1—COLLEGE INFLATION FACTORS

YEARS TO COLLEGE	6 PERCENT RATE OF INFLATION
1	1.06
2	1.12
3	1.19
4	1.26
5	1.34
6	1.42
7	1.50
8	1.59
9	1.69
10	1.79
11	1.90
12	2.02
13	2.13
14	2.26
15	2.40
16	2.54
17	2.69
18	2.85

TABLE 2— LUMP-SUM RETURN RATE FACTORS

There's no way to know for certain how much the lump-sum amount that you invest today will be worth several years from now. Still, you must assume some specific rate of return in order to estimate how much you should invest. So, we've assumed a 10 percent return-on-investment because that has been the average rate of return on the Standard & Poor's 500 Index for the past 20 years.

Now you must determine the factor by which a 10 percent rate of return, compounded every year, increases your investment. Match the correct figure from the left-hand column with the return rate factor on the right, then enter that rate on line 7a of your worksheet.

TABLE 2—LUMP SUM RETURN RATE FACTORS

YEARS TO COLLEGE	FACTOR
1	1.10
2	1.21
3	1.33
4	1.46
5	1.61
6	1.77
7	1.95
8	2.14
9	2.36
10	2.59
11	2.85
12	3.14
13	3.45
14	3.80
15	4.18
16	4.59
17	5.05
18	5.56

TABLE 3— PERIODIC INVESTMENT RETURN RATE FACTORS

Just as with a lump-sum investment, you must estimate what the value of periodic investments will be when the time comes to pay college bills. As we did in Table 2, we'll assume that your periodic investments earn a 10 percent rate of return, compounded annually. Match a figure from the left-hand column with the return rate factor to the right. Enter that rate on line 8a of your worksheet.

TABLE 3—
PERIODIC INVESTMENT RETURN RATE FACTORS

YEARS TO COLLEGE	FACTOR
1	1.00
2	2.10
3	3.31
4	4.64
5	6.10
6	7.71
7	9.49
8	11.43
9	13.58
10	15.94
11	18.53
12	21.38
13	24.52
14	27.98
15	31.77
16	35.95
17	40.55
18	45.60

Now you know the amounts you'll need to put away—either today in one lump sum or, periodically, over the years remaining until your child begins college. In the following chapter, we'll show you how you can use the tax laws to help save for your child's education.

CHAPTER 3

KIDS GET BREAKS

How much money you can afford to set aside for future college costs depends in part on how big a bite federal and state taxes take from your income. It's important to know, though, that there are ways to lower that bite while you and your child work at building his or her college war chest.

One strategy to bear in mind, no matter what kind of investment and saving program you embark on, is income shifting.

• SHIFTING INCOME

The idea underlying income shifting is simple: you reduce the family's total tax bill on money that you'll spend on college expenses by shifting some of your income from yourself to your children. How much you can reduce the family tax bill depends primarily upon the age of your child.

Children under the age of fourteen pay taxes at their parents' rate—except on the first $1,000 of income. That means you don't save much by shifting income-generating assets to your kids until they're fourteen years old.

Younger children don't have to pay any tax whatsoever on the first $500 of their unearned income. Also, the second $500 in unearned income is taxed only at the child's lower rate. So shifting some unearned income to the smaller fry will still lower the family tax bill, if only by a little.

How much could you save? Let's say that you give your four-year-old daughter $5,000, which you then invest on her behalf in a mutual fund. Over the next ten years, the fund performs well, earning an average annual return of 12 percent.

By the time your daughter reaches fourteen years of age, she will have paid just $800 in taxes on the earnings from her mutual fund. If you had paid the taxes at your, say, 28 percent marginal rate, the total tax bill would have come to $2,500.

Children who have reached age fourteen are taxed without regard to their parents' income. And your older children are usually in a lower tax bracket than you. That means income shifting makes even more sense for these children.

Let's say that your son Sam is fourteen years old and will be starting college in four years. You've already set aside $20,000 for Sam. Now you want to invest it so that while he's growing, his college fund is too. Your choice is either to invest it yourself or give the $20,000 to Sam and let him invest. If you give it to Sam, the after-tax yield on the $20,000 will be substantially greater.

Say the investment earns 10 percent per year. Over the five years, the earnings come to $9,282. But there are taxes to be paid: at 28 percent in your case, which brings the investment income down to $6,683. Sam's 15 percent marginal rate, on the other hand, reduces the after-tax earnings only to $7,890. The difference of $1,207 is the amount of taxes you'll save by shifting the income from that $20,000 investment from you to Sam.

Even if your children are still too young to take maximum advantage of income shifting, ways exist to accomplish the same end. As we discuss in the next chapter, among the investment vehicles you can use for college savings are some that are tax deferred—Series EE U.S. savings bonds, for instance. That means that no tax is due on the income earned until some later time.

Consequently, tax-deferred investments are another income-shifting device available to you. You may give them to your child no matter what his or her age. So long as the tax due is not payable until after the child attains age fourteen, the investment income will be taxed at the child's lower rate.

• GIFTS

In our example above, we suggested "giving" to your son Sam the $20,000 you had already put away for his college expenses to take advantage of his lower tax rate. "Giving," or "gifting" in tax lingo, raises the issue of gifts. Legally, without incurring a gift tax, you—or anyone, for that matter—may give Sam no more than $10,000 per year. For a married couple, the maximum gift per child comes to $20,000 per year.

But you may already spend more than $10,000 on your child—once you add up food, clothing, shelter, vacations, allowances, insurance, and so on. What's the difference between this "support" money and a gift? The IRS doesn't quibble about basic support costs. It's only when something gets excessive that the issue turns gray. Let's say, for instance, that Sam needs a car to get to and from his weekend job. You can give him a used Chevy, and that clearly counts as support. But a $60,000 BMW—*that* the government might consider a gift.

That small point aside, there's another consideration you need to think about before making large gifts to Sam: what is he going to do with the money? If you simply make him a gift outright, it's his to do with as he chooses. He could buy his own BMW instead of investing the money for college, and legally you would have no recourse.

So, in lieu of just giving Sam the cash, consider two other options: the Uniform Gifts to Minors Act (UGMA) or the

Uniform Transfers to Minors Act (UTMA). Under these laws, parents—or anyone—may give money or other assets to a child and still keep that gift under the control of a custodian named at the time the gift is made. You or any other adult can be the custodian.

There is one drawback to having the donor be the custodian. If the donor—Aunt Sally, say—dies, the gift is considered part of her estate and subject to tax if the entire estate is greater than $600,000. If the estate is worth less than $600,000, there's no problem. Or if Uncle Harry, Sally's husband, is still alive, the estate passes tax-free to him, and once again there's no problem.

There are two main differences between UGMA and UTMA accounts. The first is in how long the custodian may maintain control of the assets in the account. With UGMA accounts, the assets must be distributed to the minor—Sam, in our example—when he reaches his majority, age eighteen in most states. With UTMA accounts, however, the custodian can maintain control of the assets until Sam reaches twenty-one, or in some states, twenty-five. So a UTMA account can better help ensure that Sam uses the money as intended—to pay for his college education—instead of at his whim.

The other difference between these two types of accounts is that the UTMA gives you more flexibility in the types of assets you (or another donor) can give Sam. Almost anything, including real estate and other personal property, can be transferred into a UTMA, though you may place only cash, securities, annuities, or insurance contracts into a UGMA.

Setting up a UTMA or a UGMA and doing the paperwork is simple. The bank or brokerage house where you plan to keep the account will, in most cases, do all the work for you.

• TRUSTS

Tax laws are not the only consideration when you're trying to maximize the after-tax value of the income from investments.

If they were, trusts would be another income-shifting tactic you should consider. But, as a rule, they aren't. Here's why.

The law treats trusts differently from the way it treats individuals. If you create a trust for your college-bound child and make gifts to the trust instead of to him or her, the first $5,000 of the trust's investment income is taxed at just 15 percent. Any trust income greater than that amount is taxed at 28 percent.

Still, that's a $650 savings. If you kept the income in your own name, you probably would pay tax of at least 28 percent, or $1,400, on the first $5,000 of income. A trust would pay just $750.

The problem is that trusts require an administrator—usually a bank. And banks charge an annual fee that normally ranges between 1 and 2 percent of the principal in the trust. Usually the bank's fee will more than eat up any tax savings from the trust.

Let's say that the bank does charge 2 percent. When the principal in the trust tops $32,500, the bank fee rises above the $650 tax savings. To make matters worse, a trust of only $32,500 probably won't even earn the $5,000 required to realize the maximum tax savings. You'd be paying $650 or more to the bank and getting less than that in tax savings.

So, unless you can find a bank that charges an extremely low fee, a trust is not a good deal.

Don't be confused by terminology. The Uniform Transfers to Minors Act (UTMA) and Uniform Gifts to Minors Act (UGMA) accounts we just discussed are not trusts. They require custodians, not trustees, and there are no annual fees associated with UGMA or UTMA accounts.

• EARNED INCOME

Earned income, money paid as wages and salaries, is always taxed at your child's own marginal rate no matter what his or her age. So, if you're the owner of a sole proprietorship business, you can easily do a little income shifting from parent to child. Here's how this technique works.

You put Billy to work in your business, paying him, say, $40 a week to keep the floor of your machine shop swept clean. Those wages are earned income for Billy and are taxed at his marginal rate. Billy's wages are also a legitimate business expense to you and are, therefore, deductible from your own income. Consequently, you save twice—once by shifting $2,080 in income into Billy's lower tax bracket and second by taking the deduction from your own income.

On Schedule C of your tax return, you write off the $2,080 as wages, an allowable business deduction, and report the money as income to your son on a W-2 Form. It's as simple as that.

Child-labor laws don't apply to youngsters working in family businesses. The government's only criterion is that they be old enough to do "economically useful work," the meaning of which is not entirely clear, but the tax court has accepted as legitimate salaries paid to children as young as eight years old.

Caution: Don't try to stretch the law. The work Billy does must be real, and his wages have to be in line with what you would pay someone else for the same job. Paying him $12 an hour to sweep your floor would probably catch the IRS's attention.

And don't forget the law says that if your business is a sole proprietorship, you don't have to pay Social Security taxes on your children's wages as long as they are below age twenty-one. Corporations and partnerships, other than family partnerships, do have to pay the tax, though. In any case, your kids have to pay the Social Security tax on any wages they earn, which unfortunately, takes a bite from the income tax savings they can achieve by working for the family firm.

As a business owner you can also split income among family members, including your children, by making them partners in your business. You should know, though, that the government applies some special, strict rules to these so-called family partnerships:

The principal rule you must be concerned with says that you cannot just divide the total profits by the number of partners. The profit split must recognize the amount of the work that each partner does. For example, a mother who runs a medical transcription service makes her son a 50 percent partner in the business. At the end of the year, the transcription service has net profits of $80,000. Even though they are fifty-fifty partners, the law doesn't allow mother and son to divide those profits evenly, because the mother worked in the business while the son, a college student, did not.

The law says that some value—the wage the business would have to pay a nonfamily member to perform the same work—must be assigned to the mother's work before the remaining profits are split. In this case, let's say the amount is $30,000.

Consequently, the first $30,000 of the partnership's net income goes to the mother, then the remaining $50,000 is divided between her and her son. For tax purposes, she collects a total of $55,000 ($30,000 plus half of $50,000) and he gets $25,000—which he, of course, uses to pay for his college expenses.

Whether you employ your kids in the business or make them your partners, don't make the mistake of paying their earnings directly to their college (or to any other individual or institution, for that matter). In one case, the tax court disallowed the deduction an attorney claimed for wages paid to his children, because he had made out the checks to their colleges, not to them.

Now that you have learned about earned income and the possibilities for income shifting of unearned income, let's look at some investment vehicles you might use to build your child's education fund.

CHAPTER 4

WHERE TO INVEST
THE MONEY

Practically any sort of investment device can work in a saving-for-college program, although some have special advantages and others should be avoided.

If you're counting on this saving program to be *the* source of funds for little Susie's higher education, you want to temper the risks that you take. Investment vehicles such as commodity futures and option straddles are probably not a good idea. While they can pay big returns, losses associated with these types of investments can also quickly wipe out a modest college fund.

Being moderately risk averse does not mean, however, that you should consider only such investments as bank certificates of deposit. They're extremely safe and probably belong in any college-fund portfolio, but there is also room—as we'll discuss below—for investment instruments that promise the opportunity, if not the guarantee, of a higher rate of return.

Let's start our list of investment possibilities, however, with safety.

• CERTIFICATES OF DEPOSIT

Whether you buy them in your child's name in order to take advantage of income shifting or simply make the investment yourself, certificates of deposit, or CDs, are a useful saving-for-college device. In general, they are among the safest, if not the highest yielding, investments you can make. And, in addition, to the customary variety of CDs, there's one specifically designed for college-oriented savings. (We tell you more about this special type of CD in Chapter 6.)

Banks, savings and loans, and other financial institutions issue CDs in a range of sums with varying terms. You can and should shop around among banks before making a choice because interest rates and effective yields offered by different institutions can vary by half a percentage point or more.

The difference between "interest rate" and "effective yield" is not just academic. The yield depends on such factors as the method of compounding interest. When comparing CDs, check for the effective yield because that figure determines how much the investment will actually earn.

In shopping for CDs, you don't have to limit yourself to local financial institutions. You can buy CDs through the mail. Some brokerage houses sell bank-issued CDs, and your broker might be able to help you find a higher rate than local banks offer. Or check out financial magazines such as *Money* for listings of high-yielding CDs.

Just be wary of rates that sound too good. Institutions that offer interest far above the prevailing market rate may be having trouble attracting depositors, they might not be FDIC insured, or they may be in financial trouble. (FDIC insurance will protect your investment, up to $100,000, including the interest earned, in the event of an insured bank's failure, though your money could be tied up for a while.)

• GOVERNMENT SECURITIES

Short-term U.S. government obligations known as Treasury or T-bills are another very safe vehicle for college saving.

They come in denominations of $10,000 and up, with maturities of one year or less. You buy them directly through the Federal Reserve or through a bank or broker. (If you buy through a bank or broker, you will be charged a small commission fee.)

T-bills are sold at a discount from their face value. A one-year, 6 percent, $10,000 T-bill, for instance, will cost $9,400. But when you purchase the bill, you pay the full $10,000. Very soon thereafter, the U.S. Treasury sends you a check for $600 —the amount of the discount. Then, one year after the purchase, you get another check for $10,000—the face amount of the bill.

You can see that the interest rate you earn on a T-bill— the effective yield—is actually greater than the stated amount. In this case, it's 6.4 percent ($600 interest divided by the $9,400 you actually invested).

T-bills are a liquid investment: you don't have to hang on to them until they mature. But if interest rates have risen since you purchased your T-bill, you may take a loss on the sale.

A particularly nice feature of T-bills is that the interest they pay is not subject to state or local taxes—good news for parents living in high-tax states.

• SINGLE PREMIUM ANNUITIES

An annuity is simply a contract with an insurance company. You pay the company a single, lump-sum premium in exchange for a guaranteed payment to a named beneficiary— your son or daughter—at some specified time in the future.

The tax-saving advantage here is that the annuity's earnings accumulate tax-deferred until the insurance company begins making payments to your child. And you can time the payout to begin just when you expect college expenses to start to mount.

Caution: Check the soundness of an insurance company *before* you invest. *Best's Insurance Guide* is among the most authoritative rating services available. You can find a copy in most public libraries.

• CORPORATE BONDS

If you want higher yields than T-bills offer, you'll have to take on more risk. You get both with corporate bonds, which can also make good sense for education-related savings. Though you have to be a little more careful about what you're buying, you shouldn't rule out corporate bonds.

The U.S. Government can absolutely guarantee its obligations, because it has access to both printing presses and the taxpayers' pockets. Corporations don't have those same resources, but top-rated corporate bonds can still make good investments. Typically, their yields will run as much as 1.5 percentage points higher than those available on T-bills. You buy corporate bonds through a broker, who should be able to tell you the bonds' current Moody's and Standard & Poor's ratings. Or you can buy mutual funds of corporate bonds.

Unrated bonds, so-called junk or high-yield bonds, and those that the rating services rank low are not suitable for college-bound savers or their parents. There's just too great a chance of losing your principal or a substantial chunk of it.

Of course bonds, like stocks, do involve more risk of capital loss than investments, such as bank CDs, in the short run. If you are forced to sell a bond (or a stock) in an adverse market in order to meet an expense, you have to take the price you can get—even if it's less than the price you paid.

So, in general, corporate bonds should be thought of as long-term investments to be made when your future scholars are still young. You'll want to sell them off when you can take advantage of favorable market prices, especially as the time for paying tuition bills draws near. Then, you can park the proceeds in CDs or something else whose capital value is not subject to market fluctuation.

Caution: There is one other factor to watch out for in buying corporate bonds for college-cost investment: the call provision. This is fine print written into some bonds that allows the issuing corporation to "call" the bond (force you to sell it back) at a fixed price. A call provision gives the company the option of reducing its debt or of refinancing it at a lower cost if interest rates in general fall.

If a bond you hold is called, you will end up with cash instead of an investment paying a higher-than-market rate of interest. Then you may not be able to find the same rate of return elsewhere.

Two other variations on the common corporate bond—floating-rate bonds and put bonds—offer investors a little protection from declining bond values in a market of rising interest rates.

With floating-rate bonds, as the name suggests, the interest rate is periodically adjusted to reflect changes in the market. This feature tends to stabilize the price of the bond so that holders don't suffer the same risk of having to take a loss if for some reason they have to sell their bonds in a depressed market.

A put bond allows holders to sell their bonds back to the issuer at face value—which is not necessarily the price you paid—during certain, specified periods before the bond's maturity date. This feature also tends to keep the bond's price stable in fluctuating market—in effect, making the bond more liquid for holders. You should know, though, that in exchange for liquidity you trade yield. If you are investing for the long term, you may want to opt for a higher yield and less liquidity.

• ZERO-COUPON BONDS

These are a bittersweet dish for college-bound youngsters or their parents.

Like the T-bills we discussed earlier, zeros pay no periodic interest. Instead, you buy them at a deep discount, then, when the bonds mature, collect cash for the full face value.

You can buy zero-coupon bonds issued by the federal government through any full-service or discount brokerage firm. These bonds, like Treasury bills, are backed by the full faith and credit of the U.S. government. You can also buy zeros issued by municipalities and corporations. If you take the latter route, all the caveats that we have cited about buying only top-rated bonds apply here as well.

The sweet aspect of zeros as investments for youngsters or their parents is that they mature at a specified time, typically ten to twenty-five years from the date of issue. So you can buy ten-year zeros ten years before you expect your child to enter college and know exactly how much cash you're going to have when that day comes.

The downside to these bonds as part of a college-savings program is that although they pay no interest from quarter to quarter or year to year, the IRS requires that you pay taxes just as if they did.

One way to avoid taking this pill is to buy municipal zeros. Like the interest paid on other municipals, the interest imputed to municipal zeros is exempt from federal taxes.

As part of a college-savings program you do not want to own zeros that you know you're going to have to sell before maturity because of all bonds, zeros are the most price volatile. When interest rates fall, the market price of zeros rises more than that of other bonds. But the opposite is also true, and you don't know what rates will be when that first tuition bill comes due.

As explained in Chapter 3, children who have reached the age of fourteen enjoy some tax savings because their investment income is taxed at their rate, not at their parents'. However, the investment vehicles that follow make the same tax savings available to the younger set in one way or another. (Of course they're fine for older kids, too.)

• SERIES EE UNITED STATES SAVINGS BONDS

The U.S. government itself sells one of the best tax shelters for kids who are not yet fourteen. You can buy Series EE savings bonds in either your own name or in the name of your child.

To take advantage of the tax savings from buying Series EE savings bonds in your child's name, though, children must be at least fourteen years old when the bond matures.

The maturity period of a savings bond depends on the interest rate it pays. Bonds cost half their face value. You get the full amount when you redeem them at maturity. So the higher the interest rate, the shorter the maturity period. Bonds bought between November 1982 and October 1986, for instance, mature just ten years from their date of purchase. New rates, and thus new maturity periods, are announced by Uncle Sam twice a year. You just want to make sure that when you buy the bonds they won't mature before your child's fourteenth birthday.

The law allows you or your child to report the interest earned on Series EE bonds annually instead of waiting until the bonds mature. But there's no good reason why you would want to do so, especially since reporting the interest annually might raise the child's unearned income for the year above $1,000 and thus negate any tax savings.

Series EE bonds are sold by banks in denominations up to $1,000. To purchase bonds with larger face values, you must go through the Federal Reserve. But two $500 bonds cost no more than one $1,000 bond and buying the smaller denomination bonds lets your children cash them in gradually as they need the money. The face value of the smallest Series EE bonds sold is $50; the largest is $10,000.

Bonds cashed in before they mature earn the full rate of

interest, but the interest earned will be taxable in the year the bonds are redeemed.

You may not purchase bonds worth more than $30,000 in face value in a single year, whether you buy bonds in your children's names or give them the money to buy the bonds.

Just one other legal requirement: To buy a bond in his or her own name, a child must have a Social Security number. You may buy the bond for a child without a Social Security number, but be careful to specify that the bond is a gift. If you put your own Social Security number on it at the time of purchase, Uncle Sam will expect you to pay the taxes. When the time comes to redeem them, children will need a Social Security number to cash in the bonds they received as gifts.

Here's an even better idea when it comes to U.S. savings bonds for people within certain ranges of income—$40,000 to $55,000 for singles and heads of households and $60,000 to $90,000 for married couples filing jointly. Thanks to a break from Congress, people twenty-four years of age or older can invest in Series EE bonds issued after December 31, 1989, and use the proceeds to pay for qualified education expenses for themselves, their spouse, their child, or other dependent.

If you use the proceeds for these qualified education expenses, you don't need to pay taxes on the interest as long as the interest and principal of the bonds you redeem don't top the education expenses in any one year. This rule means it now makes more sense for you, the parent, to hold bonds earmarked for your child's education in your name.

The income ranges are adjusted annually for inflation, so if you think your income will be greater than the top of the range when your child enters college, it may make sense to put your money elsewhere—in municipal bonds, say, or nondividend-paying growth stocks.

• NONDIVIDEND-PAYING GROWTH STOCKS

Many relatively small and fast-growing companies that issue publicly traded stock don't pay dividends (and if they do, the dividends aren't very large). Instead, these companies reinvest that money back into more growth, which is good for them and could provide a tax break for your children.

Let's say that you buy one or more of these stocks in your child's name—or give the child the money and let him or her make the purchase. The child holds the stock until she or he reaches age fourteen, then sells it.

If the value of the stock has appreciated—and that's what you hope when you employ this tactic—the gain is taxed at the child's rate.

When you invest your child's money in stocks, consider using a technique known as dollar-cost averaging. It's easy. You just buy a fixed dollar amount of the stock—or of any particular group of stocks—at regular intervals. Over time, this ensures that the cost of the shares accumulated in your children's names will come closer to matching the average cost of the stock over that period than if you had bought a fixed number of shares at each purchase.

For instance, let's say you like Coopers Copper Corp. and think it would make a good investment for your daughter Sarah. Using dollar-cost averaging, you invest $1,000 in Coopers Copper on the first day of every quarter for two years. The price, in our example, keeps going up. The first time you bought it, Coopers cost $2.00 a share; then $4.00; $6.00; and finally $8.00. At the end of one year you would have spent $4,000 and bought Sarah 1,041.7 shares. That means the average cost of her shares at the end of the year is $3.84.

If you had purchased a fixed number of shares—say, 250 each quarter—instead of making a fixed dollar purchase, at the end of the year Sarah would own 1,000 shares of Coopers Copper, and you would have paid a total of $5,000. The average cost of Sarah's shares would be $5.00—considerably more than it was using dollar-cost averaging.

• TAX-EXEMPT MUNICIPAL BONDS

These bonds, issued by states, counties, municipalities, and some quasigovernmental agencies, such as turnpike or sewer commissions, are free of federal income taxes. Furthermore, if you buy tax-exempts issued in the state in which you live, there are usually no state taxes to pay, either.

Since investors aren't required to pay taxes on the interest they receive from these bonds, they're willing to accept a lower rate of interest, which in turn reduces the bond issuer's borrowing cost. In effect, the federal government is subsidizing the cost of borrowing for state and local governments.

Buying municipal bonds or shares in municipal bond funds for your kids can be a good investment. But don't make the mistake of assuming that municipals provide a tax-free ride. Though federal laws do not require the payment of tax on the *interest* income generated by municipal bonds or municipal bond funds, federal taxes do apply to any *capital gains*—either those realized when the bonds or bond-fund shares are sold or on capital gains distributions made by the bond fund.

Caution: Even shifting funds between tax-exempt municipal bond funds can generate a taxable capital gain for your child. In the eyes of the IRS, shifting funds is the same as selling the shares of one fund and using the proceeds to purchase shares of another. If the first sale results in a capital gain —that is, if the selling price of the shares is greater than the purchase price—the shift creates a tax liability. By the same token, losses realized on the sale of mutual fund shares may be used to offset gains made on other transactions or even some portion of your child's earned income.

The state tax liability on income from municipal bonds varies from state to state. Most states do not tax interest income from municipal bonds issued within that state. However, Indiana, Iowa, Kansas (on bonds issued before January 1, 1988), Nebraska, and Wisconsin do. There are even a few states that exempt capital gains earned on municipal bonds from state taxation. With the exception of Alaska, Florida, Nevada, North Dakota, South Dakota, Texas, Utah, Vermont,

Washington, and Wyoming, most states tax the interest income from municipals issued in other states. It's a good idea to check with your tax adviser on this point.

Municipal bond funds typically invest in securities offered in a number of states. This means that in filling out your children's tax returns, some interest income from the fund may be taxable in your state while some may not. The fund will tell you how its income is allocated but it's your responsibility to figure out how much of this is taxable in your state.

Your children can avoid paying state taxes on the interest income from municipal bond mutual funds if you buy them shares in funds that invest only in bonds issued in your state. A number of these state-specific funds could be useful to residents of California, Massachusetts, Michigan, New York, Ohio, and Virginia.

Before investing your child's money into any tax-exempt fund, you'll want to be sure that it makes investment sense. After all, if the interest rate on the bonds is too low, you and your kids could be better off with a taxable fund that paid higher rates.

The chart below shows you what taxable interest rate gives the same after-tax yield as a tax-exempt investment. Use it to help you evaluate potential tax-free investments.

From the top row of the table, choose the tax-exempt yield of the investment you are considering. Then follow that column down to the row that corresponds to your child's marginal tax rate. The number that you see at the intersection is the interest rate you'd have to earn on a taxable investment to net the same after-tax return as on the tax-exempt investment. (Note that this table does not take into account state and local taxes, if any.)

BRACKET	4.00%	5.00%	6.00%	7.00%	8.00%	9.00%
15%	4.71%	5.88%	7.06%	8.24%	9.41%	10.59%
28	5.56	6.94	8.33	9.72	11.11	12.50
33	5.97	7.46	8.96	10.45	11.94	13.43

If your kids can do better—that is, earn a higher yield—with a taxable investment, forget the tax-free fund. As you can see from the table, the higher your children's marginal tax rate, the better off they are putting their money into a tax-exempt fund.

You don't need the table to compare the yields of taxable and tax-free funds. You can use a simple formula to calculate the equivalent taxable yield for any given tax-exempt fund: Divide the tax-exempt yield by a decimal equal to one minus your child's marginal tax rate. And don't forget to include the state income tax rate in the marginal tax rate if your child would have to pay state taxes, too.

Say, for instance, that the tax-exempt yield is 5.75 percent, and you (and therefore your under-age-fourteen child) are in the 28 percent federal tax bracket. Divide 5.75 by 0.72 (1 minus 0.28) to get 7.99 percent, the yield a taxable fund would have to return in order to beat the tax-exempt fund. You can use the same formula to take state and local taxes into account by adding your child's state and/or local tax bracket to his or her marginal federal tax rate.

So, say you live in a state that levies a 10 percent tax on unearned income. Using the same figures as in the last example, you would have to find a taxable investment yielding 9.27 percent to better the yield of a fund exempt from both federal and state taxes. The calculation is: 5.75 divided by 1 minus the sum of 0.28 plus 0.10 $(1 - 0.38 = 0.62)$; 5.75 divided by 0.62 equals 9.27.

• APPRECIATING PROPERTY

The idea here is the same as we discussed earlier in giving your younger child shares of stock that you expect to appreciate in value. You may also give the child other kinds of property—real estate, land, stamps, coins, art, gold, and collectibles—whose value you expect to increase over time. Then, after the child turns fourteen, he or she sells the property and pays tax on the capital gain at his or her own, presumably, lower tax rate.

We've covered a lot of different ways that you or your offspring can invest the money put aside for college. But not all college expense money has to come from investments, as the next chapter will show.

CHAPTER 5

NONINVESTMENT STRATEGIES

Up until now we've been talking about ways to invest that are especially appropriate for anyone trying to get together the money for a college education.

But some techniques that don't usually fall under the investment rubric might work just as well, either alone or in combination with more conventional investments. It's okay, after all, to be creative, just as long as you know what you're getting yourself into—and, of course, as long as it works.

Here are some ideas to consider.

• ACCELERATED MORTGAGE PAYMENTS

If you have a mortgage, try fattening the check you write to the bank every month by a bit; you'll be surprised at what can happen.

Say that you buy a house when little Carol is three years old. You borrow $70,000 from the bank at 10 percent with the expectation of paying the loan back over thirty years—

bringing your monthly mortgage payment (for principal and interest) close to $614.

What if you wrote the check for $752 every month instead and applied the excess to the principal? (That's less than $5.00 extra a day.) You would pay off the mortgage in fifteen years instead of thirty. The year Carol turns eighteen and is ready to enter school, you'd have an extra $9,024 a year to spend on tuition and other expenses instead of your mortgage. (Not to mention the fact that you would have avoided paying nearly $86,000 in interest.)

Even if you can't add enough to the check to pay off your mortgage in fifteen instead of thirty years, you can probably add a little. That means that your equity will build up faster, and when Carol turns eighteen you'll have more equity in your house against which to borrow. You can then use that equity loan to pay her college bills.

• LET TENANTS PAY FOR SCHOOL

If you can afford it, rental property is another way of financing a child's education. You could consider buying some while the kids are still young.

There are two ways that rental property can help you finance future college expenses:

It is possible, depending upon local market conditions, to buy a small rental property—one with, say, three or four units —and use the rents to pay off the mortgage over a fifteen-year period. If that corresponds to the time your child is ready to start school, you now have the rental income that you were putting toward the mortgage to pay for college. And even if the mortgage isn't totally discharged, you can borrow against your equity in the apartment building.

Or, if at tuition time interest rates have declined since you purchased the building, you can refinance at a lower rate and apply the difference between your new, lower payment and the old, higher one to help defray the education costs.

Caution: You must make sure that the income from the building you purchase will at least cover your payments for principal, interest, and taxes and leave something for repairs and maintenance. If it doesn't, you'll spend more money to own the building than you realize in income.

You must also be sure you're ready to deal with the hassle of being a landlord—handling tenants and malfunctioning plumbing at odd hours of the night. If you have no experience as a landlord, talk to a friend who does.

If you do decide to go into the rental business, there's an extra little tax and income-shifting benefit to being a landlord. The kids you're going to send through college can earn extra money, taxed at their rates, by performing work at the property—doing lawn chores or making simple repairs, for instance. At the same time, you get to deduct these wages as expenses from your taxable rental income. Just be sure that the wages you pay your child are commensurate with the work done.

• COMPANY-SPONSORED SAVINGS PLANS

If the bigger problem you have is not lack of income but lack of commitment to save some of it, you might let the boss do it for you.

Many companies sponsor savings plans. If yours does, it's going to be one of two general types: qualified or nonqualified.

Qualified plans—such as 401(k) plans—involve saving money that hasn't been taxed yet. With any other plan you're squirreling away after-tax dollars. The problem with qualified plans as saving-for-college devices is that you usually can't get your money out without a penalty until you reach age fifty-nine and a half. But there is a way around that problem.

Most companies allow you to borrow against your savings for education expenses. Before making any assumptions, though, talk to your personnel department to see what sort of rules, terms, and restrictions apply in your company.

With nonqualified plans, getting at your money is not an issue. You've already paid taxes on the money contributed to the plan and on the plan's investment earnings, so you're free to withdraw it as you will.

There are two nice features about company-sponsored savings plans. One is that they relieve you of having to write a check every week or every month. Saving with a company-sponsored plan is as painless as saving gets. The other nice bonus is that some employers may match what you contribute. They may match dollar for dollar, or perhaps they put away only $1.00 for every $2.00 of yours, but it's still a great deal. Where else can you get an immediate 50 percent return on an investment?

• GIFTS FROM GRANDPARENTS

If your children's grandparents are wealthy enough—and willing—they can pay some or all of the kids' college expenses by making periodic gifts of cash or securities to the children. Birthdays are a good time for this gift-giving. The only limit here is the $10,000 cap on tax-free gifts per year per giver. Grandma and Grandpa together, of course, can give up to $20,000 a year. Gifts can also be small and frequent—however you and the children's grandparents think it will work best for them and for you.

• SYSTEMATIC SAVINGS

Whatever happened to plain old thrift—putting a little bit aside every week or every month? It still works.

If you can put away just $10 a week, about $1.43 a day, and invest it at a 10 percent annual rate, after eighteen years you'll have accumulated, with earnings, $26,326. Twenty-five dollars a week invested at the same terms will see you with a $65,816 balance.

If periodic savings just isn't your style, think about one-time savings. If you can scrape together $1,000 on the day little Stephanie is born and put it someplace where it will earn 10 percent annually, then when Steph is seventeen and ready for college, she'll have a $5,054 head start. Saving that way is almost painless.

In the next chapter, we'll look at a newer way of "saving" for college expenses—prepayment programs.

CHAPTER 6

PAY NOW, LEARN LATER

Many colleges, including some state institutions, will give bargain tuition rates to students who pay early. There are advantages, to be sure, to these "tuition futures" or "guaranteed" tuition plans, but there's plenty of risk as well.

• WHAT ARE PREPAYMENT PLANS?

Prepayment is a recent innovation among college financing plans, and it initially received a good deal of favorable publicity. However, prepayment is not for everyone, and some plans aren't as good as others.

There are three different kinds of prepayment plans, each with its own variations. Some are operated by specific colleges or universities—college-based plans; some are operated by states; and others, private plans, are operated by banks or other financial institutions.

They are great schemes; it's just not always clear who benefits.

• WHAT DO YOU NEED TO KNOW ABOUT COLLEGE-OPERATED PREPAYMENT PLANS?

These plans, like all the rest, are based on the principle of the time value of money, which says that a dollar in hand today is worth several dollars received some time in the future.

With prepayment plans, colleges are saying that if you give them a lump sum now, they'll give your child a tuition-free education in the future. How much you have to pay in this bargain depends on the school's current tuition rate and on how early you make the payment. With state schools, the size of the payment also depends on your residency.

If you decide to prepay when Junior is sixteen years old, just two years away from entering school, the lump sum will have to be quite large—perhaps nearly four times the school's current annual tuition charge. If you make the lump-sum payment the day Junior is born, you may pay just one year's current tuition charge.

In other words, something in the neighborhood of $8,000 to $10,000 paid today might guarantee your newborn tuition-free schooling when he or she is ready to matriculate eighteen years later. If room and board and other fees are included in the prepayment plan, the required payment will be substantially larger—roughly double.

Not every school or institution offering the prepayment option requires a single lump-sum payment. Some will accept installments. But they're not giving anything away. Money paid later buys you less future tuition benefit.

• WHAT ARE THE DRAWBACKS OF THE COLLEGE-BASED PLANS?

Beware of deals that sound too good to be true. For just a little bit of money now, the prepayment plans promise, you'll never have to worry about college costs again.

Maybe, but . . .

What if you pick a school now and Junior picks another school eighteen years later?

What if Junior doesn't qualify for admission to the school you chose?

What if the school shuts its doors for financial or other reasons between now and then?

What if Junior decides not to go to school?

In most cases, you'll get your money back—but only the money you paid in, possibly a bit more.

Prepayment plans don't operate like normal investments that earn interest or dividends for you over time. If the schools pay any interest at all on your money, it's at a very low rate.

In addition to all their other drawbacks, prepayment plans can make you ineligible for any other financial aid that you might have received.

Our advice: don't get involved in these very early college-based prepayment plans. The security they offer is appealing, but too much can go wrong. Besides, you can get the same security by taking the cash you would spend on the prepayment and putting it instead into a high-yield investment. The money is still yours, it generates regular income that you can allow to accrue, and it's all available to you any time you want it.

Most important, without the prepayment plan you don't have to make decisions about what school your children will attend before you—or they—can possibly know.

• TWO COMMON VARIATIONS ON THE COLLEGE-BASED PLANS

With the first, you make a lump-sum payment but not until after Junior has been accepted to the school and has decided to go. Then you pay for all four years' tuition, and, for paying early, the school gives you a discount.

You've reduced the risks of prepayment substantially, because Junior has, after all, been admitted, and the school is still there. But you haven't *eliminated* the risk. What if Junior wants to drop out? Change schools? What if he flunks out? What if the school drops the major study program Junior signed up for?

You'll get a prorated portion of your payment back, but without interest.

This type of prepayment plan is still fraught with risk. And like the other college-based plans, we advise you to avoid it.

One other variation on prepayment does, however, bring the risk down to a reasonable level. In this variation, you pay tuition annually but from one to several months in advance. Early payment earns you a discount from the school with the risk that Junior may drop out, flunk out, or transfer. You may get some part of your payment back, but again, unadorned by interest. Just make sure that the discount offered makes even this small risk worthwhile. You might still be better off leaving the money in an interest-earning investment account until the bill actually comes due.

• ARE STATE-SPONSORED PREPAYMENT PLANS ANY BETTER THAN THE COLLEGE-BASED KIND?

In some respects, they are. But because these plans vary so much from state to state, generalizing about them is difficult. Currently only Florida, Indiana, Maine, Massachusetts, Michigan, Tennessee, and Wyoming either already have a plan or are talking seriously about creating one.

Your best approach to deciding whether to participate in one of these plans is to go to the appropriate state financial aid agency armed with a rigorous set of questions.

You'll want to ask about payment options. Find out whether you have to make a single, lump-sum payment or can pay in monthly or annual installments.

Because tuition charges vary for in-state and out-of-state

students, find out what the plan requires. Do you and your child have to be state residents? What if you move after you've made the payment? What, specifically, are the residency requirements?

Some plans cover only tuition charges. Others cover fees and room and board as well. Some apply only to undergraduate tuition. Some will take your child through graduate school. You must find out exactly what costs are covered by the plan.

Some states allow only parents and children to contribute to their prepayment plans. Make sure you know what restrictions your state applies. Generally, though, they don't have to cause a problem. If Grandma wants to contribute and the plan won't allow this, she can make a gift to you or your child that can then be put into the plan.

A big issue with any plan is how you get out of it if you or your potential scholar has a change of heart. If you want to withdraw, how much of your investment can you get back? With interest? How much interest?

The plan might allow you to transfer the benefit you've purchased to a private school within the same state or to a public or private school in some other state. Or it might allow no transfers at all. This is a key point. And if the plan does permit transfers, what, exactly, is the value of the benefit that you'll receive when the tuition bills come due? Some states pay the other school only the tuition charged at their own state university. You, your child, or financial aid must make up the balance due.

Sometimes students drop out of school for a semester or a year. Sometimes they skip a year between high school and college. Sometimes they want to study part time for a while. What provisions has your state prepayment plan made for accommodating these changes of plans?

Some state plans impose time limits on students. They may, for instance, pay for only four years of college. What if your child wants to take longer—five years, say? Or what if your child wants to shorten his or her college career by studying through the summer? Will the plan pay?

Maybe you have two kids and the older one changes his or her mind about school. Will the state plan allow you to transfer benefits from one to the other?

Finally, figure out what the actual yield on your money is with the state plan. It's easy to estimate. You know how much you have to pay. Then check the rate at which costs at public colleges and universities have been rising for the past few years. Extend that rate of increase ahead to the year that your child will enter school to get the estimated cost then. Now compare your required payment to that projected cost. What's the effective interest rate your payment is earning? Could you do better just by investing the money in a CD or a mutual fund?

Although these state-sponsored prepayment plans may offer advantages over the college-based variety, all the same caveats that we raised earlier still apply. Prepayment reduces or eliminates the financial aid your child may be eligible to receive. Consequently, the plan may actually cost all but wealthy parents and children more than it saves them. Also, be wary of state plans that limit your child to attending in-state schools only. That means that your child loses flexibility of choice.

If there are so many drawbacks to these plans, why did they elicit so much positive response when they were first conceived? It's because they do offer parents protection from dramatic increases in the cost of education. But so do private prepayment plans, which let you retain a great deal more flexibility in the choice of schools and the timing of your child's education.

• WHAT ABOUT PRIVATE PREPAYMENT PLANS?

These come in many varieties, and they all have the advantage over college-based and state-sponsored plans of not restricting your choice of schools. But as you examine these plans the questions you should ask in every case are the same: what is the yield on the money I put into it? Am I better off making another investment?

Private prepayment plans in general take one of two shapes. One looks much like a bank Christmas club. You begin making regular payments at some point before your child enters school. The amount of the benefit that you eventually reap depends on the size of the installment payment, how long you make it, and—as we said—the rate of interest paid.

The other type of private prepayment plan is nothing more than a variable rate certificate of deposit (CD). In this case, the rate of interest paid on the CD is tied to some indicator of the rate at which college costs are rising. The College Savings Bank in Princeton, New Jersey, offers one of the better known of these CDs.

The bank calls this certificate of deposit its CollegeSure CD. It's not intended as a short-term parking place for money, but as a vehicle for long-term savings for college. The CollegeSure interest rate can change annually, based on what happens to the "Independent College 500 Index."

Calculated and published by the College Board, this index tracks the rate of change in tuition, room and board, and fees paid by full-time freshmen at 500 private four-year institutions of higher learning. On July 31 of each year, the College Savings Bank pays interest on your CollegeSure CD at a rate one point lower than the Independent College 500 Index. (If the amount in your CD is less than $10,000, the interest earned is one and one-half points less than the index.) In the unlikely event that the rate of inflation in college costs drops dramatically, the CollegeSure CD is guaranteed to pay a minimum rate of 4 percent.

Like most other bank CDs, this one is FDIC insured. It's also top-rated (AAA-L) by Standard & Poor's. You can pick a maturity anywhere from one to twenty-five years.

The minimum initial deposit in a CollegeSure CD is $1,000, but you can make subsequent deposits of $250 or more. You can buy these CDs through the College Savings

Bank or through several large brokerage houses. You may withdraw the interest from a CollegeSure CD at any time without penalty, but if you want your principal back before maturity, you'll have to pay a penalty fee of 10 percent during the first three years or 5 percent during any other year except the last year, when it drops to just 1 percent.

It's hard to say whether the CollegeSure CD will be a better investment than a conventional CD—or even as good. In general, these CD-type plans are good as long as college costs grow faster than the rate of interest you could earn on a normal CD or another financial instrument.

These privately offered prepayment plans have the same disadvantage as the others in that they reduce or eliminate need-based aid that you otherwise might receive.

• WHAT ARE THE TAX IMPLICATIONS IN CHOOSING AMONG PREPAYMENT PLANS?

States and the federal government tax the earnings of private and college-based prepayment plans just as they would other, similar investment income.

The tax treatment of state-sponsored plans, however, is different. The IRS has ruled that no tax is due on interest earned in the Michigan prepayment plan—one of the first of its type in the country—until a child actually begins to attend school. Then, the child, not the parent, owes tax on the difference between the amount of money contributed to the plan and the value of the charges the plan actually covers.

The tax isn't due all at once, though. Rather, it is spread out over the years the child receives benefits from the prepayment plan. Say, for instance, you contribute $10,000 to the plan, which your child uses to pay for four years of tuition charges that come to $20,000. In each of those four years, your child is taxed on $2,500 income from the prepayment plan. How the federal government will tax plans that differ significantly from the Michigan plan remains to be seen.

Also, state taxes on proceeds from their own prepayment plans vary. As a rule, states will build tax incentives into the plan to encourage their use. For instance, Michigan lets taxpayers deduct the contributions they make to the state's prepayment plan from their taxable income.

We've now covered your options for squirreling away money *before* college bills come due. In Part II, we'll examine the choices you have when it comes time to pay those bills.

WHEN THE BILLS ARE
UPON YOU

CHAPTER 7

WHAT NOW?

Whether you've planned or not, the time is here. Junior's college is going to expect a check soon for the first semester tuition, fees, room, and board.

What do you do?

More well-to-do people may take the money right out of their incomes. The rest of us have three funding sources from which to draw, and most parents draw from all of them: borrowings, savings, and financial aid. We'll look at all of these options in the chapters ahead.

In this chapter, we want to give you some perspective on borrowing.

• SHOULD I BORROW?

There's absolutely no shame in borrowing to cover educational expenses, but there can be plenty of pain in the paying back.

That's the principal caveat in tapping credit to help cover

the cost of college educations: don't get yourself—or your kids, if they're the ones who'll be doing the repaying—into a deeper hole than you or they can crawl out of. In general, you want to minimize the amount of your loans, borrowing no more than you absolutely need. Then you want to look at every lending source available to you and at every type of loan. Some cost more than others. Some come with strings that you might not want attached.

• HOW MUCH DO YOU NEED TO BORROW?

If you've done your estimating and calculating well, you know how much you'll need, and borrowing more than that amount just to have a cushion can run up your expenses.

On the other hand, don't borrow less than you need and can afford to repay. Of course, children can work and help to pay for their schooling, but the point of college is to study, not to sling burgers. Too much time on the job can seriously disrupt a student's academic life.

Students who borrow themselves must do so with a clear appreciation of what will be required to repay the loan—and when repayment has to start. Unpaid student loans can prove a heavy burden to carry into the first years of a career.

• HOW MUCH CAN YOUR CHILD REPAY?

If Junior has a career already in mind, the high school guidance counselor or college placement officer should be able to help you "guestimate" his future earning capacity and, therefore, his ability to repay the loan.

To figure out the repayment requirements, talk to people at the college financial office or your local bank. They deal with loans daily and can give you at least an estimate of the monthly payment required.

• WHAT ASSUMPTIONS SHOULD YOU MAKE?

None. A loan is a legal, binding contract, so make sure you and your child thoroughly understand everything about it. This is no time to be shy about asking questions.

We've heard of students who thought they were obtaining grant money but were unwittingly taking out a loan. Sometimes, too, students don't realize they will have to make out several separate checks each month if they take out more than one loan. They mistakenly assume that someone will consolidate all their debts into one repayment package when they graduate.

So you and your child should never assume. Instead, pin down the answers to these important questions:

What is the interest rate on the loan or loans? Is it fixed over the life of the loan or is it variable? If it varies over the life of the loan, to what index is it pegged—one-year Treasury-bill rates? Two points above the prime rate? (The index can make a big difference in the rates your child will pay in the future.)

Again, with a variable rate, your child should find out how frequently the rate changes and by how much. Is there a cap on the rate—that is, can it go only so high and no higher? If your child takes out a loan without a cap, he or she is asking for problems.

As for the repayment schedule, inquire how long the repayment period is and how much each monthly payment will be? What about fees? Is there an origination fee paid when the student takes out the loan? What about service fees or charges to ensure that your child will pay back the loan.

Does the loan carry any restrictions? Does the lender have the right to call it in before its due date? What circumstances would trigger such a call?

If the loan is canceled, what notification will your child receive? Do prepayment penalties apply if the student pays off the loan before its due date? Is the loan a balloon? In other words, will your child have to make a large lump-sum payment when the payment schedule expires?

Ask what happens if your child falls behind in his or her payments. Might the lender have the right to garnishee your child's wages? What would trigger that action? (We think, by the way, that it's a poor idea to take out a loan that does allow wage garnisheeing.)

• WHAT INTEREST IS FULLY DEDUCTIBLE?

Alas, interest is fully deductible on only one type of loan that you take out for educational purposes—the loan that's secured by a mortgage on your primary residence or second home.

The tax code, however, has some strict rules you must meet before you may deduct interest you pay on second mortgages and on home-equity loans.

The law says that you must take out the loan either on your primary residence or on a second house—a vacation home, for example. Also, the loan proceeds must be clearly slated for education. If the loan amount doesn't go toward meeting educational or medical expenses, the amount you can borrow on which interest remains deductible cannot exceed the amount you paid for the house plus the cost of improvements you have made to it. Equity loans taken out to pay educational or medical expenses, on the other hand, can top this amount, and the interest remains deductible.

For example, say you purchased your house for $50,000, and have $40,000 outstanding on your mortgage. Over the years, you've sunk an additional $50,000 into improvements. The market value of your house has soared over the many years to $200,000. Now you want to use some of your equity to help finance Junior's college bills.

No matter what you use the money for, you could still deduct any interest you paid on a home-equity loan of up to $60,000—that is, the $50,000 purchase price plus the $50,000 in improvements, less the $40,000 outstanding on your mortgage. However, if you borrowed more than $60,000, you could only deduct the interest expense on this additional amount if you use the loan proceeds to meet educational or medical expenses.

The rules say you must also incur the educational (or medical) expenses within a reasonable time before or after refinancing your home. Otherwise Uncle Sam may say that you're using the money for some other purpose, and you could lose the deduction.

Caution: Second mortgage or home-equity loans have other nondeductible expenses attached to them. For example, banks often demand that you pay points or "loan origination fees," just as you would if you were buying a property. And, likewise, there are often closing costs to add in. These "extras" could end up costing you several thousand dollars—all nondeductible—when it comes to using your home to finance college expenses.

These additional costs aren't the only drawback to borrowing against your house to finance college expenses. If you take out a home-equity loan with a variable rate (one that floats with the market), your monthly payment could increase beyond your ability to pay it.

• WHAT INTEREST IS PARTIALLY DEDUCTIBLE?

If you don't, or can't, take out a home-equity loan, your other borrowing choice is a personal loan. Whether you take the loan from Aunt Sally, your bank, a college, or the government, it is personal. That means the interest you pay is personal interest and completely nondeductible.

Don't rule out a personal loan to finance education costs just because the interest is not deductible. Just be aware of what the real cost of the loan is when you compare alternatives.

•SHOULD YOU LOAN MONEY TO YOUR CHILDREN?

Maybe you have enough money available to pay for your child's education. However, you think that Jane should shoulder some or all of those costs herself, so you loan her the amount she needs to pay for college. And say you decide not to charge Jane interest. After all, she is your own flesh and blood. That's perfectly all right with the IRS, but Uncle Sam may require that you "impute"—or assume—interest income from the loan, even though you never see a cent.

The rule is if you loan your child $10,000 or more, you must report to Uncle Sam imputed interest that comes to the lesser of the amount of the outstanding loan times the applicable federal rate (a rate based on what the federal government pays to borrow) or the net investment income of the borrower if it tops $1,000.

This regulation isn't really that complex. You just obtain the applicable federal rate for the period in question—your tax adviser or banker will have it—then multiply the loan amount by that rate. Then you compare this figure with the investment income your child reports on his or her tax form for the year.

Here's an example. Say you loan Jane $30,000 interest free. The applicable federal rate comes to 9 percent. So the annual interest you must impute could be as much as $2,700 ($30,000 times 9 percent). However, if Jane has no investment income for the year, your imputed interest also comes to zero.

If Jane earned $2,000 from investments? You have to claim that amount in imputed interest. If her investment income is really large—$6,000, say—you must claim the full $2,700 as imputed interest income. (Of course, if Jane's investment income were that great you probably wouldn't have to loan her money anyway.)

You can avoid the imputed interest by charging Jane a market rate of interest. If you do, of course, you're adding that sum to your income.

The bottom line: Look carefully at the tax consequences of your borrowing or lending.

Now that you know some of the consequences of taking out loans, let's look at some specific loans, beginning with those offered by Uncle Sam.

CHAPTER 8

ON THE CUFF

Plenty of government-backed borrowing opportunities are available to parents and their college-bound youngsters. This chapter will tell you where they are.

One caveat before we begin. Defaults on government student loans have been running from 20 percent to 40 percent in the last few years. In fact, some commentators have compared the problems with government-backed loans to the troubles that beset the savings and loan industry. So don't be surprised if these loans become much less common in future years.

• PERKINS LOANS

Perkins loans take their name from the late Kentucky congressman and longtime chairman of the House Education and Labor Committee Carl D. Perkins.

A Perkins loan is made by the federal government to a

qualifying college or university. The school, in turn, loans the money to its undergraduate (and graduate students) deemed to be in need of financial assistance.

Perkins loans were designed to encourage students to enter a number of low-paid professions, such as working with the handicapped or with children in Head Start programs. If a graduate pursues one of these careers, his or her Perkins loan is usually totally or partially forgiven. Perkins loans, or National Direct Student Loans, as they used to be called, carry an unusually low interest rate (5 percent in 1991).

Any undergraduate student who seeks a degree at an accredited institution and whom the school judges to be in need is eligible for a Perkins loan. Many colleges and universities make Perkins loans only to full-time students.

Uncle Sam allows eligible students to borrow as much as $9,000 over four years—$4,500 for students in a two-year degree-granting program. Graduate students may borrow no more than $18,000, which includes any Perkins loans they may have taken out as undergraduates.

Each school sets its own deadlines for Perkins loan applications, usually early in each calendar year. Students should apply as soon as possible. Once approved for a Perkins loan, a student gets his or her money only after signing a promissory note agreeing to repay the debt. The school will either pay students directly or credit their accounts in at least two payments.

Most schools require borrowers to begin repayment six months after graduation—or immediately if they become less than half-time students. Repayment can stretch over as long as ten years. The amount of the monthly payment depends on the size of the loan and the length of repayment period but usually may not be less than thirty dollars per month.

However, the school can reduce or even waive this minimum payment if a borrower becomes ill or unemployed for a long time. The school can't forgive the loan, but it can extend the repayment period if other circumstances make repayment on the original terms difficult.

To get some idea of the interest charges you'll incur with a Perkins loan and the size of the monthly payment you'll have to make, consult this chart:

LOAN	NUMBER OF PAYMENTS	INTEREST	MONTHLY PAYMENT	TOTAL REPAID
$ 4,500	120	$1,227.60	$ 47.73	$ 5,727.60
9,000	120	2,455.20	95.46	11,455.20
18,000	120	4,910.40	190.92	22,910.40

Don't forget that graduates who enter certain typically low-paid professions, such as teaching in Head Start, can expect a reduction or forgiveness of their debt.

Repayment deferral or partial forgiveness is also available to graduates serving in the U.S. armed forces, Peace Corps, Vista, or branches of the U.S. Public Health Service. Bankruptcy is another means out of paying the Perkins loan debt—but only if the borrower has been making payments on the loan for at least five years. Also, a school may forgive the outstanding loan balance if a borrower dies or becomes disabled. If you have questions about whether you qualify for a repayment deferral or partial forgiveness, check with your school's financial aid office.

If someone becomes delinquent in making Perkins loan payments, a school may demand immediate repayment of the entire outstanding balance plus all interest and penalty charges. If full repayment isn't made, the school can sue. Furthermore, it can ask for help from the federal government to collect what it's owed.

It's not a good idea to default on a Perkins loan. A defaulter's consumer credit rating will take a beating, because the school or the government will almost certainly report the default to the credit bureaus. And anyone defaulting may end up repaying the loan anyway, because the IRS can seize income tax refunds and use them to reduce the balance due on a delinquent Perkins loan.

• GUARANTEED STUDENT LOANS

Guaranteed Student Loans—GSLs, for short—are loans guaranteed by the federal government but made to students by banks and savings and loans. GSLs aren't available through college or university financial aid offices. Schools have nothing to do with these loans.

With a GSL—or Federally Insured Student Loan, as they are sometimes called—Uncle Sam pays the interest while the borrower remains in school and for six months afterward. The government also guarantees the lender that the loan will be repaid. GSLs are made to students—not to parents—and students are obligated to repay the amounts they borrowed.

Although the interest rate on GSLs is lower than the market rate, it's higher than the rate charged on Perkins loans. Currently, the rate for new borrowers is 8 percent for the first four years and 10 percent thereafter.

Undergraduates may borrow up to $2,625 annually during their first and second years in school, and up to $4,000 annually in their third year and beyond. But under no circumstances may an undergraduate's GSLs add up to more than $17,250.

Graduate and professional students may borrow as much as $7,500 per year—up to a maximum of $54,750 for undergraduate and graduate loans combined.

In the old days, any student whose family reported an adjusted gross income of less than $30,000 qualified for a GSL. The loan covered what educators called a student's "remaining need"—that is, the cost remaining after the family had made its contribution and after any other financial aid.

But the 1987 Higher Education Act changed all that. Nowadays, just having a low family income doesn't automatically qualify anyone for a GSL. All applicants must submit to a complicated financial needs test. The test takes into account such factors as assets, savings, income, number of children in the family, and number of children in college.

But even showing need is not enough. Beyond the second year of school, GSL recipients must demonstrate academic proficiency, too. Their grade point average must meet the school's standards for graduation.

Moreover, GSL borrowers pay a 5 percent origination fee that's similar to the "points" that lenders levy on home mortgage loans. The bank subtracts this fee from the amount borrowed. Say a student wants a $2,000 GSL from an institution that imposes a 5 percent origination fee. He or she pockets only $1,900—that is, the $2,000 loan minus a $100 (5 percent) origination fee. Out of that $1,900 the borrower must also pay a 1 percent insurance fee to the federal agency that's guaranteeing the loan, bringing the usable balance down to $1,880.

Applications for GSLs are available from banks, savings and loans, and other participating lending institutions. Completed applications should be mailed to college financial aid offices, which must verify the information before the lender can process the application.

If the college or university that the borrower plans to attend participates in the so-called Pell program (more on this topic in Chapter 11) the financial loan office there must determine whether the applicant is eligible for a Pell grant before he or she can receive a GSL.

The loan approval process for a GSL can take as long as six weeks, so prospective students should begin looking for a lender soon after being accepted by a school. Besides, just completing the loan application is going to take a bit of time.

The loan can come from a bank in the state where the borrower lives or plans to go to school. However, not all banks and financial institutions participate in the GSL program, so students can contact their school's financial aid office or the state agency that guarantees these loans as a proxy for the federal government to receive a current list of lenders.

The really tough part of a GSL, like any loan, is paying it back. The government says that the lender must allow borrowers at least five years to clear the debt and that it *may* allow as many as ten. Repayment begins immediately after graduation—or after a student drops out of school or begins attending less than half time.

Under some conditions, repayment of a GSL debt may be postponed or the loan forgiven altogether. The rules here are similar to those for the Perkins loans we discussed earlier. One notable exception: certain categories of teachers, such as those working with the handicapped and health care workers, don't get the same full or partial forgiveness of their GSLs as of their Perkins loans.

As with any debt, the size of monthly payments will vary with the amount borrowed and the time allowed for repayment. But with GSLs, there is a minimum: $50 a month or $600 a year. Prospective borrowers should find out from lenders what their payments will be before deciding to take out the loan. That news can have a sobering effect on the most enthusiastic would-be debtor.

Use this chart to get an idea what payments would be with various-size loans. The chart assumes an 8 percent interest rate.

LOAN	NUMBER OF PAYMENTS	INTEREST	MONTHLY PAYMENT	TOTAL REPAID
$ 2,500	60	$ 541.46	$ 50.69	$ 3,041.46
5,000	60	1,082.92	101.38	6,082.92
10,000	120	4,559.31	121.33	14,559.31
12,500	120	5,699.14	151.66	18,199.14
25,000	120	11,398.28	303.32	36,398.28

Just as with Perkins loans, delinquent GSL borrowers can expect lenders to demand immediate payment of the entire loan. The government can sue to collect the balance due on a loan in default, and it will notify credit bureaus. Likewise, the IRS will seize any tax refunds due until the GSL debt and accrued interest have been repaid. Not unexpectedly, the federal government withholds any other student aid from individuals who haven't made arrangements satisfactory to the government to repay their GSLs.

• HEAF PARENT LOANS (PLUS) AND SUPPLEMENTAL LOANS FOR STUDENTS (SLS)

These are both loan programs for individuals who don't meet the needs tests required to qualify for Perkins loans or GSLs. As their names suggest, the PLUS loans are made available to parents of college-bound children. SLSs are loans to the kids.

Both PLUS and SLS loans carry a variable interest rate that changes yearly. To find out what the current rate is, you can ask a participating financial institution or the college financial aid office.

Some limits apply to each of these programs. Students may borrow no more than $4,000 for each year they are in school. The entire SLS loan may not exceed $20,000. However, taking out an SLS loan does not count against a student's GSL loan limit.

Parents' PLUS loans are also limited to a maximum of $4,000 per year and $20,000 in total. But parents may borrow this amount for each child they have in school at least half time.

The application process for these loans is much the same as for GSLs except that you don't have to demonstrate financial need. The bank, credit union, or savings and loan to which you apply will run a credit evaluation on every applicant. Although they don't charge points or an origination fee on these loans, lenders may charge an insurance premium of as much as 3 percent of the loan, which will be taken out of each disbursement they make.

Repayment begins almost immediately with these loans, although each is a little different. PLUS borrowers—parents, that is—must begin repaying interest within sixty days of receiving money from the loan. SLS borrowers—students—must begin paying interest on the amount borrowed within sixty days. Repayment of principal is deferred until after borrowers finish school, drop out, or become less than half-time students. However, at the lender's option, SLS and PLUS interest payments may be deferred if the borrower asks.

Loans such as the ones we've just described can prove a valuable way to pay for college. But, instead of borrowing, maybe you can tap some of your assets instead. We'll address this option in the next chapter.

CHAPTER 9

TAPPING ASSETS

Part of the cost of covering college expenses will probably have to come from your assets—savings you have put away and investments that you've made. For some people, it's simply a matter of going to the bank and withdrawing the cash.

But most of us don't keep our savings in cash. Our nest egg may be in the form of real estate or financial securities. In this chapter, we'll show you two ways you can turn assets into cash or use them to acquire the money you need to keep the bursars off your back.

• TAPPING THE EQUITY IN YOUR HOME

If you're like most people, the largest asset you have is the one you return to each evening—your home. Tapping the equity you've built up in that asset is certainly one way to go when it comes to paying college expenses. As we saw in Chapter 7, you can take out a second mortgage or a home-equity loan, use the proceeds for educational expenses, and deduct all the interest on this loan, even if the amount tops the cost of your house plus improvements.

Of course, there's no good reason to take out more than you need. Instead of getting a chunk of money all at once, you might instead establish a home-equity line of credit, which you can then use when your child has expenses coming due. With this approach, you pay interest only on the amount you must use, not on the total sum available.

Whether you take out a second mortgage, a home-equity loan, or a line of credit, don't be shy about asking your banker for the most flexible repayment terms you can get. You should make sure, for one, that your loan carries no prepayment penalties, because adding just a few extra dollars in principal payments each month can save you a substantial chunk of money. It can also slash the time it takes to repay the loan.

• TAPPING APPRECIATED STOCK

Maybe when your child was just an infant, you invested in some shares of a growth stock, hoping it would appreciate nicely. Your strategy paid off, and the value of your stock has soared. You're now ready to sell the shares and use the proceeds to pay for your child's education. But wait. It's a better idea to transfer title to the shares to your child and let him or her sell it. Your child can then apply the money to educational expenses.

The advantage of the transfer: your child will pay money on the big appreciation in value of the stock at his or her rate, not yours.

Example: Say, when daughter Sally was only two you bought $4,000 worth of shares in XYZ Corp. Now Sally is college-bound, and the value of the shares has grown to $30,000. You give yourself several pats on the back for your shrewd investment, then sell the stock for a hefty $26,000 profit. But since you're in the 28 percent tax bracket, you must shell out taxes of $7,280 on your gain, leaving you $22,720, not $30,000, for Sally's college fund.

So let's try an alternative approach. You transfer the shares to Sally's name, and she sells them. Your daughter is only in the 15 percent tax bracket, which means Uncle Sam takes a $3,900 cut from her profits, and you collect an additional $3,380 that can now be applied toward Sally's college expenses.

There's just one potential pitfall to this approach. Once you transfer shares of stock—or any other asset—to your child, those assets are his or hers. Your son or daughter can sell them and do whatever he or she likes with the proceeds. If Junior would rather take off and explore Europe than go to college, that's up to him. You no longer have control over the money.

Maybe your child's education—or part of it—can be financed without anyone's having to take a loan or liquidate assets. In the next chapter, we'll look at scholarships available to students.

CHAPTER 10

WHY PAY IF YOU DON'T HAVE TO?

S weet, sweet scholarships. They pay so you don't have to. And where do you find these marvelous devices? Lots of places.

Here are the basics, followed by a plan for scouting them out.

• WHAT ARE SCHOLARSHIPS?

Scholarships are gifts, often with strings of one sort or another attached.

The characteristic that distinguishes scholarships from grants is that, typically, they aren't based on need, but on some other criteria—academic or athletic achievement, for instance.

• HOW DOES YOUR CHILD OBTAIN A SCHOLARSHIP?

Scholarships don't seek out students; students have to search for them. The variety of organizations and institutions offering scholarships of one sort or another is truly astonishing.

Some available scholarships award almost trivially small amounts of aid while others will pay for an entire four-year education. The challenge is first in locating the scholarship source, then in meeting its criteria. In this chapter, we will help you with the first of those problems.

• WHERE DO I START LOOKING?

Sit down with a pencil and paper and start making a list.

To what organizations do you or other members of your family belong? Begin with community or civic and business groups, such as the Rotary Club and the Chamber of Commerce. What about fraternal organizations, such as the Elks or Moose? Do you—or your child—belong to a union? What about your church, and if not the individual congregation, what about the denomination?

Think of clubs and organizations in which your child has been active: 4-H, Boy Scouts, or Girl Scouts. A father's college fraternity or mother's sorority might offer help to members' offspring.

Think, also, about specific interests your child has, such as the law, science, the environment, or mathematics. Then think of organizations that support or promote those interests, such as state bar and medical associations or national conservation groups.

Your child's school guidance counselor is likely to have a list of *some* scholarship opportunities, but you can be sure that there exist more possibilities than appear on that list.

Once you've drawn up your own list of possibilities, we suggest that you or your child contact the organizations and inquire. Some you may want to telephone. For others, a letter from your child might be more appropriate.

If your child writes, he or she should make the letter brief. It should simply state who the child is, the nature of the affiliation (or the parent's affiliation) with the organization, what school he or she expects to attend and when, and the prospective plan of study. Then your child should ask whether there are scholarships available for which he or she might be eligible. Don't send a form letter, and make sure the letter that goes out is grammatically and typographically accurate. You or your child can follow up on the letter by phone.

• DON'T SOME EMPLOYERS OFFER SCHOLARSHIPS?

You bet they do, and you shouldn't neglect this potential source. Some employers provide scholarship aid to employees' children.

If your child has a job, he or she should inquire about scholarships from that employer.

And if your child doesn't have a job but is thinking of getting one, even a summer job, he or she might let scholarship availability be one of the criteria used in deciding where to apply.

Here's another idea: Some companies allow employees to take college courses while they are employed, and they frequently pay for those courses. Sometimes they require that the study relate to the employee's job skills at least remotely, but sometimes they impose no such requirement. Your child should inquire. It can't hurt.

• YOU MEAN MY CHILD DOESN'T HAVE TO *NEED* THE HELP TO GET A SCHOLARSHIP?

Very few students couldn't use a little help with college expenses, even if they don't qualify for needs-based assistance.

But as we pointed out earlier, most scholarships are based on merit. Does your child excel at running, swimming, writing, painting, acting, music, sculpting, raising animals, or growing plants? There is probably a scholarship created for him or her. But your child will most likely have to compete for it.

The National Merit Scholarships is just one—and probably the best known—of the many merit scholarship programs. Some colleges have their own merit scholarship programs, and the availability of this kind of scholarship might influence your child's choice of schools.

• CAN'T SOMEBODY ELSE DO THE LOOKING FOR US?

We've already suggested that *one* place to start looking for scholarships, after you and your child have exhausted your own imaginations, is the high school guidance office.

Computerized scholarship search services are also available, and the guidance counselor should know about them. Your child fills out a form describing himself or herself and his or her interests. The service feeds this information to a computer, which then comes up with a list of scholarships for which your child might be eligible. You should be aware that the fee for this service may run as high as $100.

We can't recommend any particular service, and one caution is in order: guidance counselors and financial aid officers say that these services aren't especially helpful in providing information that is not available elsewhere free.

• CAN MY CHILD GET BOTH FINANCIAL AID AND A SCHOLARSHIP?

Yes, but he or she may not be able to keep it all.

The fact that your child is receiving a financial aid package from the college won't prevent him or her from winning a scholarship that is not based on need. If your child does win a scholarship, however, he or she will very likely have to give up part of the aid package. The first part of the package that the school is likely to take back is any grant assistance it has offered.

Don't let the possibility of losing some financial aid deter your child from pursuing a scholarship, though. Winning one will establish your child as a desirable student, which may induce the college to offer a better aid package in the long run.

• WHAT ABOUT THESE STRINGS THAT YOU MENTIONED?

Many scholarships do require something of your child once he or she has agreed to take the money. They might require a student to participate in a specific sport or to perform on a particular musical instrument. Some, such as the military scholarships that we'll discuss in Chapter 13, require a certain amount of summer time as well. Some scholarships require maintaining a minimum grade level in order to continue eligibility. Others might demand that a child take particular courses or stay within a specific major.

These requirements shouldn't deter anyone from seeking a scholarship, but students should be realistic about their desire and ability to conform to these requirements. An athletic or music scholarship, for instance, may demand more time practicing than academic studies will allow. Students can find themselves in trouble later as a result of conflicting demands.

The best list of scholarship possibilities is the one you and your child make after consulting as many sources as you can think of and exploring your own imaginations.

Scholarships are a boon, but so is financial aid. In the next chapter, we'll look at the financial aid packages available and how to apply for them.

CHAPTER 11

ONE FORM FITS ALL

Actually, there are two standard financial aid forms. But no matter how many colleges, public or private, your children want to apply to, they have to fill out these forms only once.

In this chapter, we'll tell you what happens to these financial aid forms and how to be sure you position yourself best to take advantage of the help that's available.

•WHO SHOULD APPLY FOR FINANCIAL AID?

Almost everyone ought to complete the financial aid forms— even the children of parents who are very comfortable with their bank accounts. Even if you make too much money or have too many assets to qualify for need-based financial help, there are other reasons to go through the trouble (and it is a major chore) of filling out the financial aid forms once. Many loans, on-campus student employment, merit grants, certain discounts, and prepayment programs require the form.

Don't assume that your child is not eligible for aid. Also, don't let false pride deprive you of the benefits that aid can bring. Fill out the forms and encourage your child to apply for everything he or she is eligible for. It can't hurt.

• WHAT ARE THE BASIC REQUIREMENTS FOR RECEIVING AID?

Naturally, every organization, institution, or program that offers student aid has its own eligibility criteria, so you'll have to consult their literature or representatives. However, much of what you'll want to know will probably be included in the package of financial aid information and forms that your child's high school guidance department should provide. It's important to reemphasize that almost all aid programs still require students to complete the standard financial aid forms.

• HOW DO YOU APPLY FOR ASSISTANCE?

The application process for college financial aid is long and complex. Many steps can't be taken until other steps are completed. Some steps must be taken before admission; others can be taken only afterward. It's probably going to take you and your child hours to complete all the forms. Furthermore, they're intrusive: they ask all sorts of questions that usually are no one's business but your own. You'll probably get bored, frustrated, and confused.

We tell you all this now so that when it happens, you won't be surprised. When you (parent and/or child) ask a school for an application, along with it will probably come a package of financial aid material. It will include information and forms for aid from the U.S. Department of Education, the state, and from the college itself.

Be sure to locate the aid form in the application material

and look for the submission deadline. In most cases, parents must sign this form before it is returned to the school.

Timing is important. In no case, unless the school specifically asks for it, should financial aid applications and the accompanying information be sent to a school before January 1 (assuming that your child is seeking fall admission). However, no matter what the stated submission deadline, your chances of receiving aid are better the sooner you apply for it. Our advice: it's an onerous process that doesn't get any easier, so get your financial aid forms in to all the schools to which you are applying as soon after the first of the year as possible.

The basic aid package that the school sends you will take care of most, but not all, financial aid for which you might want to apply. It does not cover PLUS or SLS loans, personal loans, or some student employment programs. Neither does it cover special aid programs offered, for instance, by employers or unions or by civic, religious, or cultural organizations. These all require separate applications. Often your child's high school guidance counselors can help identify these programs, but even they can't keep track of all of them. Applications for aid from these specialized sources should be submitted at about the same time as your basic aid package.

PLUS and SLS loan applications aren't submitted until after your child has accepted admission to a college. Likewise, you can apply for discounts and incentives only after admission because they are available only to enrolled students.

You're not locked into an aid package, even after it has been offered. If your financial circumstances subsequently change, or if you can show that the aid offered does not accurately respond to your need, the package can be revised.

Important: Your child must apply anew each year for financial aid the following year.

•MUST YOU SUBMIT YOUR TAX RETURNS?

The colleges will want tax returns for the most recent year, which means that you're going to have to complete your returns much earlier than you may be used to. Colleges will want to see complete tax returns—the Form 1040 and all the schedules you're required to attach to it—for parents and for the child applying to school. If parents file separate returns, both must be submitted. Requirements vary from school to school for divorced or separated parents. It will be clear on the financial aid application. Most schools will also ask for an accounting of nontaxable income, if any.

Because you want to file your financial aid application as soon after January 1 as possible, you might want to ask your employer in December for help in getting your W-2 form early. But you don't have to wait for these before filling out your return. The information on wages paid and taxes withheld is available to you long before the forms are. And, if necessary, you can send your returns in without the W-2s and then submit them later.

In fact, it may even be permissible and desirable to submit an estimated tax return if by doing so you can get your financial aid application in early. Check with the school first to see if it will permit you to follow up with the actual figures later.

Note: Just because colleges want to see your tax returns as early in the year as possible doesn't mean that you actually have to file them or pay any tax owed before the official April 15 due date.

•WHAT EXPENSES DO YOU LIST?

All of them.

In general, the more information you can provide a college's financial assistance office, the better the aid package it is likely to offer. You'll want to fill out the schools' financial aid forms as thoroughly and as accurately as you can. Filling in all the blanks may require you to do some research or make some calculations. Take the time to do it.

When the forms ask you to list expenses, put it aside, and make your own list of expenses, then fill in the forms' blanks later. Start your list with ongoing expenses that apply both to you and/or your child. Begin with the easy ones: mortgage and car payments, food, clothing, insurance, utilities. Don't leave anything off just because it's small—the monthly cable TV charge, for instance. Lots of small things can add up to a big chunk of change.

Next start a list of irregular, infrequent, or special expenses—everything you can think of. Maybe one of your children is going to need braces next year. What's that going to cost? Do you need to paint the back porch? What about the cost of airfare to check on the health and well-being of your aging parents? Do you own a dog or cat? Pet food and care cost money. Will you be purchasing a personal computer for your college-bound child? Put it down.

List every conceivable expense and an explanation of that expense if it isn't obvious. Explain briefly, for instance, *why* it's desirable or necessary for you to visit your aging parents twice a year.

Now, return to the form and fill in all the blanks presented. You'll find that a great many of the expenses on your list are not suggested by the questions posed on the financial aid form.

After you have completed the form, list any expenses not covered there, along with their explanations, on a separate sheet of paper and attach it to the form when you submit it. Some college financial aid officers may ignore your attachment, but for others it will provide a more complete understanding of your financial picture to help them justify the best financial aid package they can offer you.

Careful: The separate list we just suggested should be attached to the financial aid forms you send to each college to which your child is applying. It should not be attached to the comprehensive aid forms that we are about to discuss. (Those don't go to the colleges, and nothing beyond what is asked for should be submitted with them.)

• WHAT OTHER FORMS MUST YOU FILL OUT?

Besides sending in financial aid applications to the schools to which your child applies, he or she must also file at least one or two of the following comprehensive aid forms:

—The *Family Financial Statement* (FFS), which the American College Testing Program (ACT) publishes and processes.
—The *Financial Aid Form* (FAF). This form is published and processed by the College Scholarship Service (CSS), a division of the College Entrance Examination Board, which is also know as the CEEB or College Board.
—The *Student Aid Application of California* (SAAC)
—The *Application for Pennsylvania State Grant and Federal Student Aid*. This so-called PHEAA form is published by the Pennsylvania Higher Education Assistance Agency.
—The *Application for Federal and State Student Aid* (AFSSA), published by the Illinois State Scholarship Commission.

Be forewarned. All these forms are long and require that you supply a lot of information about your family's finances, including income, assets, and debts. Of course, you can make any large purchases that you were going to make anyway shortly before signing the form. That way you lower your assets by the amount the purchases cost. Doing so is perfectly legitimate since you're listing assets and liabilities that are current as of the date you sign the form. All these forms, which are very similar, ask you for your actual income during the previous year and an estimate of the income you expect to have during the current year.

While these forms are tedious and demanding, you can use them to apply for the U.S. Department of Education's need-based financial aid programs, financial aid from colleges themselves, and, in most cases, aid from states as well. Each school to which your child applies will let you know the form it requires or prefers, and each college requires that you file only one of them.

If the school's financial aid office lets you know that it has a preference for one form over another, send in the one it prefers. Not only will cooperating give the college exactly the data it wants, it will show those in charge that you and the prospective enrollee are serious about receiving financial aid and that your son or daughter is eager to gain admission.

Except for the FAF and FFS, these forms don't cost any-thing to file. You can request them from your child's high school guidance office, which will make them available to col-lege-bound students free of charge. You can also request forms from the college's financial aid office.

The forms change from year to year, and it's important that your child use the current one; colleges won't accept older versions and you may miss the submission deadline.

The U.S. Department of Education publishes another com-prehensive form, the *Application for Student Aid* (AFSA). It resembles the forms we just listed. It, too, is free, and can be obtained from college financial aid offices and high school guidance offices. However, the AFSA form is useless unless you're applying for USDE aid programs, which the other forms cover as well. (We'll explain USDE programs shortly.)

When should you mail these forms? You must sign and mail each to the appropriate processing centers no earlier than January 1 of the year in which your prospective student would like to begin school. (You'll find the address of the processing center on the instructions that come with each form.)

Take care not to sign or date the form in the previous year: If you do, the form won't be processed, and you'll have to start all over again.

So complete, sign, and mail these forms as soon as you can *after* December 31. Some schools provide only a small window during which they must receive the forms, asking for them as soon as February 1, or even January 15.

You'll notice that some of these comprehensive forms ask if your child wants to apply for USDE aid, which is sometimes referred to as a "Pell grant" or "federal aid." **It's important to say "yes" if the form asks.** If your child replies in the negative, the school's financial aid office may disqualify him or her for this aid.

The good news? Parents and children have to complete a comprehensive aid form only once a year, no matter how many schools the child applies to. You can send the data from each form to as many colleges as your child would like. Just list the schools in the appropriate spot on the form. Naturally, though, if you have another child who wants to go to college the following year, you must mail a separate comprehensive form for that child.

It takes about three to six weeks for the center to process a comprehensive aid form. When it is finished, the processing center produces a *Student Aid Report,* which outlines the finances of your family and suggests the contribution your family should make to your child's education for the academic year ahead. A copy of this report is mailed to you and to the financial aid officers of the schools you designate.

The suggested contribution is not final. It's the amount the processor determines that you and your child together should be able to contribute toward meeting the total cost of your child's attending school for the year. The financial aid officer is perfectly free to boost or cut the amount the report suggests when he or she actually makes a financial aid award. So you shouldn't try to negotiate with the financial aid office now—even if the suggested contribution seems enormous. Wait until the financial aid office makes its decision. Your family contribution may be lower than you anticipated.

• DOES YOUR CHILD QUALIFY AS AN "INDEPENDENT" STUDENT?

This is a child whose parents no longer claim him or her as a dependent on their federal and state tax returns. Independent students don't have to include any information about their parents' income, assets, or debts on any of the comprehensive aid forms. However, some colleges do ask for parental financial information on their own financial aid forms. If they want it, even independent students must supply this information to the schools.

• SHOULD YOU FILE A FORM
WITH THE STATE?

Your child will likely want to apply for state aid as well—and that requires filling out more forms. (Note that aid from the District of Columbia and U.S. possessions is considered "state" aid when it comes to financial aid for colleges.)

Make sure that your child applies to state-sponsored financial aid programs if he or she applies for admission to any school, public or private, in his or her home state. However, it's important to realize that your child may be eligible for state aid from his or her home state (and, in some cases, from another state), even if he or she has applied only to out-of-state colleges. You might have to call or write each of those states' financial aid agencies to see exactly what programs, if any, your child will be eligible for at the schools there. This aid varies from state to state.

Also some states—Connecticut, for example—require you to file separate financial aid applications on top of the colleges' aid applications and the comprehensive forms. Other states—California, Illinois, and Pennsylvania are three of them—have sensibly combined the state and comprehensive forms into a single form. Still other states don't require you to fill out a special form at all. In these states, you automatically get the state financial aid mechanism going when you apply for financial help at any college in the state.

Many states make the process easier for you and your child by including a state aid application as part of the FAF and/or FFS. If you live in Ohio, for example, you would file a special Ohio version of the FAF or FFS, which you can obtain from high school guidance and college financial aid offices throughout the state. When you file an Ohio FAF or FFS, you have automatically filed an application with the Ohio state aid agency for financial assistance.

You fill out a generic comprehensive form in those states that don't combine their financial aid application with a comprehensive form. The FAF generic version is known as the *National FAF;* the generic FFS is called the *Regular FFS.*

• ANY TIPS ON APPLYING FOR FINANCIAL AID?

The most important advice is worth repeating: make sure that you take the time to fill out all financial aid application forms as completely, carefully, and accurately as you can. You're only creating extra work for yourself if you don't.

If you leave out some data or fill a form out incorrectly, your child's application won't be processed. That means, of course, that you'll have to submit it again. The result: you'll lose precious time, since the forms take several weeks to process. So check each form carefully, then check it again—even check it a third time.

A second piece of advice is also worth repeating.

Make sure you're completely honest when you fill out the forms. Any information you put on the form may be checked. If you should deliberately supply false or misleading information, you may disqualify your child from receiving any financial aid. What's worse, deliberately supplying false or misleading data can result in a fine or even a jail sentence.

You should also fill out all parts of any financial aid form. Don't refuse to fill out sections. If you do, your child, again, may not be able to receive aid.

Of course, it always makes sense to photocopy every form you've completed and store the photocopies in an easily accessible place. That way if a form you mail goes astray—or a number somehow gets scrambled—you'll have a copy close at hand. It's also a good idea to make sure the financial aid forms you sent arrived safe and sound. So wait a few days after you've mailed a form and call the school or send the form return receipt requested.

You shouldn't request a receipt when mailing a comprehensive or state form. Doing so only slows down the processing. Send these forms by regular first-class mail. After three weeks have passed, call to see if the comprehensive form has been processed and if a *Student Aid Report* was sent out. Don't be shy about calling again if a *Student Aid Report* hasn't arrived six weeks after you mailed a comprehensive aid form.

You also should have no hesitation about getting in touch with a college's financial aid officer if you have any questions or concerns. He or she will be happy to answer your questions; it's part of the job.

In the next chapter, we'll look at another alternative to funding a college education: working.

CHAPTER 12

WORKING IT OUT

A s a way to finance some or all of the cost of a college education, getting a job is a time-honored strategy. While the idea isn't new, collegiate job seekers do have several advantages working for them: good placement services, flexible hours, hiring preferences, and wage subsidies that can make them awfully attractive to potential employers.

Not every student should work, and those who do have to be careful about allocating their time and energy between their jobs and studies. But it's the rare student who can't devote *some* time to a job if he or she needs the income. In fact, some students find that having a job makes them better students because it forces them to organize their time.

A job can be part of the aid package offered by a college or university. If it's not, there are usually still campus jobs available and jobs in the community for students who want to work.

In this chapter, we'll tell you about the kinds of jobs students are likely to find on or near campus and how to go about finding them.

We'll begin with work-study jobs and service awards

which are likely to be part of any financial aid package your child is offered. Then we'll cover the kinds of jobs that students have to hustle strictly on their own.

• WORK-STUDY

Work-study jobs usually don't pay much more than the minimum wage. Often they don't involve very exciting work: food service, clerk-typist, maintenance, reception, and so forth. But they are usually close, convenient, and tailored to a student's schedule.

Look through the information in the financial aid package for anything about a work-study "grant" or "scholarship" of, say, $2,000. What it's really offering is a work-study job at which your scholar can earn up to $2,000 a year. Just because the aid package talks about work-study, though, is no guarantee that the school will be able to find your child a job. Nor does it mean that your child has to take the job that's offered or assigned. Declining all or part of a work-study job won't jeopardize the rest of a student's aid package. And students can quit a work-study job partway through the school year, also without jeopardizing any other aid they may be getting.

The only drawback to not accepting a job or walking away from work-study work is that you have to make up the cash somehow—maybe with a bigger loan or maybe with a better job outside of the work-study program.

Plenty of students who aren't getting financial aid take work-study jobs when they're available. Some colleges will give first priority for these unclaimed jobs to students who already have work-study but need more. Some give priority to students who applied for but were turned down for aid, while others just put them up on a first-come, first-served basis.

Part-time students are eligible for work-study jobs, too.

The clearinghouse for work-study jobs varies from school to school. It can be the financial aid office, the office of student affairs, or the student employment office. Don't worry. It'll be easy to find, but more often than not these jobs can't be arranged until after students get to school.

Work-study wages get paid just like any other wages, and they are taxable, too. So, if your son's or daughter's financial aid package mentions a $2,000 work-study "grant," that's in pretax dollars. It won't pay $2,000 worth of tuition or fees, which, unfortunately, come denominated in after-tax dollars.

• SERVICE AWARDS

With service awards, we can be talking real money: seven to fifteen dollars an hour, maybe even more. But we're also talking skills and limited availability. Service awards include assistantships and fellowships. They are almost always academic-related and involve work such as research, teaching, or assisting professors. Sometimes academic secretarial work is also included in the assistantship category as well as in work-study.

In any case, these positions are terribly difficult to get because most of them are reserved for graduate students. The handful of undergraduate service awards are often reserved for a select few: officers of the student government or the editors and staff of the school's newspaper, yearbook, or literary magazine.

• STUDENT EMPLOYMENT OFFICE

Practically every college or university has some sort of student employment service, even if it's only a bulletin board where outside employers can post available jobs. The employment office will often act as a locator of off-campus jobs available from firms of all types. Some will actually set up application appointments for job-seeking students. This office may also be the place students can find out about on-campus jobs that don't fall into the work-study or service grant categories. Usually, student employment offices don't discriminate among full- or part-time students or students with or without financial aid.

Often students can find or sign up for temporary, short-term work through the employment office. The office will maintain a list of students desiring short-term work and the kind they want to do. Then, when a business or a local resident needs someone to, say, cut the grass or take inventory, they can call and get the names of interested students.

• OUTSIDE EMPLOYMENT

However the student employment office works at your child's school, a word about outside employment is appropriate.

These jobs usually pay more than the available work-study jobs, and they have other advantages as well. They may last through school vacations and summers, when the other jobs don't. They frequently offer the potential for advancement, which is hardly ever the case with on-campus jobs. Sometimes these off-campus positions can lead right in to a postcollege job.

The downside is that off-campus employers are less interested in your child's education than in getting a job done. They may put pressure on their employee—the child you sent off to study—to work harder or longer than is consistent with his or her concurrent need to be a student.

• CREATING A JOB

Student entrepreneurs have become a growing phenomenon on campus. Students have done everything from selling magazine subscriptions, setting up pizza delivery services, creating a catering service, tutoring, typing papers for other students, or even selling computers. Maybe your child can create something on his or her own that could teach valuable skills and even serve as a springboard for a career, once the student graduates. The other advantages to these entrepreneurial ventures are that the student sets the hours and is his or her own boss.

• INTERNSHIPS

An internship with an outside organization is another route students can take when it comes to finding work. Colleges offer these internships on either a part-time or full-time basis. Some internships pay salaries and nearly all grant academic credit. Internships can be valuable, because they can provide your child with experience and insight in a field that may interest him or her.

So your child should check to see if the school in which he or she is interested has a special internship office, or if it runs programs through the student employment office, career placement office, student affairs or student services offices, and/or individual departments.

Internships don't have to come only through established internship programs, either. Students often arrange internships on their own by simply contacting organizations in which they're interested, then finding faculty members who are willing to serve as sponsors.

Financial need doesn't play a part when it comes to internships. They're open to nearly all students, though sometimes the school restricts them to upperclassmen.

To find out about internships, your child can look in one of several books published each year that list many of the internship opportunities around the country. The current edition of *Internships: On-the-Job Training Opportunities for All Types of Careers* (Peterson's Guides, Inc., Princeton, N.J.), for example, contains nearly 40,000 listings, and this list is far from complete.

• COOPERATIVE EDUCATION

Cooperative education, which is also known as co-op education and co-op jobs, is becoming increasingly popular. These programs combine regular academic study with on-the-job experience and training in a field in which the student has an interest. Co-op jobs always pay salaries, sometimes good ones, and often the college will give students academic credit when they work in these programs. Also, these jobs often provide a terrific opportunity for after-graduation employment. (Close to 40 percent of all co-op students continue to work for their co-op employers after they graduate.) Qualifying for financial aid is not a prerequisite for participating in co-op programs. In some programs, students go to school for one quarter, then work full time for the next.

Cooperative education gets its biggest boost from the federal government, which offers thousands of co-op jobs. Many other organizations also sponsor co-op programs, though, so look around. To explore these programs, your child should contact the director of cooperative education at the college through either the co-op office, the internship office, the student employment office, the job placement and planning office, or the student affairs or student services offices.

Your child can also obtain information on co-op programs by writing to The National Commission for Cooperative Education (360 Huntington Avenue, Boston, MA 02115, or calling the commission at [617] 437-3778). It will send at no charge some general information on co-op education, a list of co-op programs in the United States, and a list of colleges that offer cooperative education. A book called *Earn & Learn* is also a valuable resource for finding out about co-op jobs, programs, sponsoring agencies, and participating colleges. You can obtain a copy for $4.25 postpaid by writing to Octameron Associates, Box 3437, Alexandria, VA 22302.

Are there any other ways to obtain aid? You bet. If your child is the least bit militarily inclined, the U.S. armed services offer some super deals. In the next chapter, we look at these options.

CHAPTER 13

HUP, TWO, THREE, FOUR

The Air Force, Army, Navy, and Marines all have Reserve Officer Training Corps (ROTC). ROTC students get full tuition, books, and fees as well as a small monthly paycheck. Of course, there's a cost.

First, you have to find a school that has an ROTC unit. Then you must qualify academically and pass a rigorous physical exam. Once you're in, you must participate in weekly ROTC classes for at least two of your four college years. And, once you've graduated, you must serve a minimum of six years in the service, four of them on active duty.

The armed services also offer other programs that can help slash college expenses. Let's begin, though, with ROTC.

• WHAT IS ROTC?

ROTC is the most popular military financial assistance program available for college students.

ROTC programs come in three types. The first pays all or

nearly all college expenses. The second pays a monthly stipend. The third pays expenses plus a monthly stipend. All three programs require students to participate in ROTC training.

ROTC scholarship recipients—called cadets by the Air Force and Army and midshipmen by the Navy and Marines—must take elective courses in military science while they are in college. These courses needn't affect the student's academic major, however. In addition, ROTC cadets and midshipmen participate in weekly drills and attend a summer training program. The drills typically last only a couple of hours, and the summer training still leaves students with some vacation time. ROTC students wear their uniform during drill periods, but otherwise they're civilians, indistinguishable from their non-ROTC classmates.

In exchange for meeting these requirements, cadets and midshipmen on full ROTC scholarships receive:

• compensation for all tuition and academic fees and for textbooks costs
• a tax-free monthly stipend of $100
• salary of approximately $400 per month while engaged in summer training
• a travel allowance from home to college when the student first starts school
• free space-available flights on military aircraft
• free uniforms

Added together, these goodies can be worth more than $50,000 over a four-year scholarship. But besides the study and drill requirements while students are attending school, ROTC scholarship recipients make a major commitment in agreeing to serve on active military duty after graduation.

The competition for ROTC scholarships, which are awarded annually, is fierce. Only one in five seekers is selected, and the selection is based on more than just academic accomplishment. The services do consider SAT and ACT scores and class standing, of course. But they are looking for future officers and leaders, so they also consider the applicants' roles in athletic and extracurricular activities.

• Do all schools offer ROTC?

Some do, some don't, and some let you go elsewhere for it.

Those schools that do participate do so either as "host" or as "cross-enrollment" institutions. Host schools have active ROTC units on their own campus. Cross-enrollment schools allow their students to go to a nearby host school's campus to take part in ROTC instruction and drills.

The Army's is the largest of the three service ROTC programs. It has approximately 300 host schools and more than three times that many cross-enrollment institutions. Next is the Air Force with 150 host colleges and universities and 650 that permit cross-enrollment. Navy (which includes Marine) ROTC scholarships are available at 65 host schools and 115 cross-enrollment institutions.

• Where can I obtain additional information on the ROTC programs?

For information on Air Force ROTC programs: Air Force ROTC, Public Affairs Office, Maxwell AFB, AL 36112-6663. For information on Army ROTC programs: Army ROTC, P.O. Box 9000, Clifton, NJ 07015-9974.

For information on Navy or Marine ROTC programs: Navy-Marine Corps NROTC Scholarship Program, P.O. Box 3060, Hyattsville, MD 20784.

• IF I HAVE TO SERVE IN THE MILITARY ANYWAY WITH AN ROTC SCHOLARSHIP, AREN'T THE MILITARY ACADEMIES A BETTER DEAL?

Financially, you're right. Midshipmen at the Naval Academy in Annapolis, Maryland, the Merchant Marine Academy in Kings Point, New York, and the Coast Guard Academy in New London, Connecticut, and cadets at the Military Academy at West Point, New York, and the Air Force Academy in Colorado Springs, Colorado, get a four-year college education absolutely free. In addition, academy midshipmen and cadets are paid a salary that's greater than the stipend received by ROTC scholarship students.

One problem with the academies is that there are fewer slots available each year than there are ROTC scholarships. Another potential drawback to attending an academy is that some courses of study aren't available.

Many appointments to all but the Coast Guard Academy are made through nominations by U.S. representatives and senators. But several categories of appointments don't require congressional nominations. The academies' admissions office can tell you about those. Coast Guard Academy appointments are made through a national competitive examination.

For more information, write: Director of Admissions and Registrar, United States Military Academy, West Point, NY 10996; Director of Admissions and Registrar, United States Air Force Academy, Colorado Springs, CO 80840; Superintendent (Attention: Candidate Guidance), United States Naval Academy, Annapolis, MD 21402; Director of Admissions, United States Coast Guard, New London, CT 06320; Director of Admissions, United States Merchant Marine Academy, Kings Point, NY 11024.

Remember that the academies now accept women as well as men for education and subsequent military service.

• WHAT IF I DON'T WANT TO BE AN OFFICER?

No problem. Going into the military can still help you pay for a college education. You can start that education while you're in the service, or you can attend college just as if you were a regular civilian, once you've finished your hitch.

While you're still serving, there is something called DANTE—the Defense Activity for Nontraditional Education Support. DANTE allows servicemen and -women to earn college-level credits by taking correspondence courses.

If you actually want to go to class while you're still in the service, you can do that on an off-duty basis at many military bases. Some of the on-the-job technical training that you receive from the military may also earn you some college credit later on.

A recruiting office can give you the lowdown on educational opportunities for military enlistees. Don't be nervous about going into one: They won't trick you into signing up.

If you do sign up, however, and complete your military obligation, you may be eligible for a great deal of financial assistance with college expenses after your discharge. In 1985, Congress created a new GI Bill, which replaced the existing Veterans' Educational Assistance Plan (VEAP).

You "may" be eligible, because you have to decide whether or not to participate. If you think you might want to go to college after getting out of the service, the new GI Bill allows you to accumulate benefits in an "education account." Service personnel who elect to participate have $100 a month deducted from their service pay during their first year of duty. That gives you $1,200 in your education account. Depending on how long you serve, the government can add as much as $9,600 more to that account.

Again, check with a military recruiting office to find out the very latest information on the new GI Bill.

• WHAT IF I AM ALREADY A VETERAN? CAN I GET FINANCIAL HELP?

Maybe. Go or write to your local Veterans Administration Office. Someone there will be able to answer your questions or point you in the right direction to get answers.

• SO THE MOST FINANCIAL AID I CAN GET AS A FUTURE SERVICE VETERAN IS THE $10,800 FROM MY OWN CONTRIBUTION AND THE GI BILL?

No, that's not the case. The Army has an additional program that it calls the Army College Fund. Depending on how long you serve, the ACF can contribute as much as another $14,400 to your education kitty, which means that all together, between the GI Bill and the ACF, you could have as much as $25,200 to help ease you through school after a four-year Army hitch. In two years, you could accumulate as much as $17,000; in three years, as much as $22,800.

• HOW DO I QUALIFY FOR THE ARMY COLLEGE FUND?

The Army uses this program as an incentive to get people to train for critically needed positions within its ranks. These are jobs such as food service specialist, metal worker, and power generator equipment repairer. You must serve at least twenty-four consecutive months before you are eligible to receive any part of the government's contribution to your ACF.

• How do I get my Army College Fund money after I serve?

It comes to you through the Veterans Administration in monthly installments so long as you are enrolled full time in an approved college program. (Most college programs qualify for VA approval.)

The size of the monthly check you get from the VA will depend on the total amount in your education account. But let's say that it's the maximum of $25,200—$1,200 that you contributed, plus the $9,600 government contribution plus $14,400 from the ACF.

Every month that you're a full-time student you'll receive $700. Here's how the VA calculates that amount: First, it takes the total amount in your account—$25,200, then divides that sum by thirty-six months (the total number of months the government figures it takes to complete college—four academic years of nine months each). You can see from this math that you won't be receiving benefits during the summer months when school is not in session.

If you attend school for only two years, you will still have eighteen months' worth of benefits remaining in your account. If you go to school only part time, the VA will reduce the amount of your monthly check, but will pay you for more than thirty-six months.

So long as you are enrolled in a qualifying educational program, you're entitled to whatever money is in your education account. And the amount of money you are eligible to draw from this account monthly is not diminished by any other financial aid you might receive.

Caution: You must use your GI Bill and Army College Fund benefits within ten years of your discharge. After that time has elapsed, you lose any funds still remaining in your account.

• WHAT IF I'VE ALREADY GRADUATED FROM COLLEGE BUT NOW I'M STUCK PAYING OFF MY LOANS?

There's an Army program for you, too.

If you took out a National Direct Student Loan or a Guaranteed Student Loan after October 1, 1975, the Army will help you pay it back—at a price. The price is that the Army wants you. For every year you enlist and serve, the Army will reduce your loan debt by one third or $1,500—whichever is greater. Serve for three years, and your loan is repaid. Serve for two, and you've wiped out two thirds of it or $3,000 worth.

But, you say, you didn't go to four years of college, so that you could spend the next three years in the Army. Okay, don't, but you can still get help with your debt. If you sign up for the reserves, the Army will repay 15 percent of your loan or $500, whichever is greater, for every year of reserve duty.

You probably won't have to give up your career—just a weekend a month and two weeks every summer. Do this for six years, and you'll wipe out 90 percent of your education debt. One caveat, though: as the 1991 war in the Gulf showed, reservists are subject to being called up for active duty when the need arises. So make sure you understand this possibility when you sign up.

Once again, check with an Army recruiter for more information on the Army's loan-repayment program.

• DO ANY OF THE OTHER SERVICES OFFER MORE THAN THE BASIC GI BILL?

Yes, they all do.

• WHAT IF I WANTED TO JOIN THE MARINES?

The regular GI Bill benefits apply in the Corps, of course, and the Marines offer four other programs. Two will help you get college credits while you're serving in the Marines. The other two will help you get a full college education plus a commission as an officer in the Corps.

First, there's the Tuition Assistance Program. The Marine Corps will pay 75 percent of the cost of college courses taken during off-duty hours at an accredited institution. You may also use the program to help pay for qualifying correspondence courses.

The Continuing Education Program involves several accredited universities that guarantee that military transfers over which you have no control won't cost you credit or time lost. These universities allow you to take regular classroom courses and correspondence courses and to receive college credit for some military training.

If you want to become an officer in the Corps, the next two programs apply.

Enlisted Marines who can show a selection board that they were educationally deprived or "culturally differentiated" before entering the Corps can take advantage of the BOOST (Broadened Opportunity for Selection and Training) program.

This program amounts to a year's prep school study to get the enlistee ready to compete for a slot at the U.S. Naval Academy or accepted into the Marine Corps Enlisted Commissioning Education Program (MCECEP), the second program leading to an education and an officer's commission. In MCECEP, which is open to active duty and reserve Marines, you attend a ten-week prep school, then you're sent to one of thirty participating universities where you go to school full time. The main difference between a regular student and a Marine in MCECEP is that the Marine isn't paying for his or her education and is receiving full pay and allowance all the time.

After college, graduates attend normal Officers Candidate

School and then receive a commission as a U.S. Marine second lieutenant.

• What special education deals does the U.S. Navy offer?

The Navy's principal college education program for enlisted personnel is called Navy Campus. It is, so to speak, a college away from college.

With Navy Campus, enlisted personnel can study during off-duty hours to earn the same college credits that civilians on campus earn. Courses are taught ashore at naval bases and even at sea on board Navy ships. The Navy, like the Marine Corps, subsidizes the cost of these courses and helps its personnel continue their college courses despite the disruption of military transfers.

If you stay at it long enough, you can earn a full college degree through the Navy Campus program. If you want to become an officer in the Navy and go to college full time, there are two programs for that, too. Essentially, they work just like the Marine Corps BOOST and MCECEP programs that we have just described.

Qualified enlistees can go to prep school to bring their academic skills up to the point that they can compete for admission to a civilian college or for appointment to the U.S. Naval Academy. Once they're in school, they receive full Navy pay, allowance, and benefits. Those who attend the Naval Academy will get their ensign's commission immediately upon graduation. Those who go to civilian universities will be commissioned after attending Officers Candidate School.

The Certificate Degree Program (CDP) is one other opportunity to receive a college degree under Navy auspices, and this doesn't require that you remain in the service to get it. In the CDP, you can receive a full degree from a participating college or university without ever taking courses on its campus. The school, in essence, agrees to accept for credit courses that you take at other, accredited institutions in pursuit of a particular course of study to which you and the school have agreed. With CDP, you can begin your college career while you are still in the Navy and continue it even after leaving the service, as long as you complete it within ten years of starting.

One other special educational deal works for you in the Navy—Service Members Opportunity Colleges (SOCNAV). In SOCNAV, Navy enlisted personnel can earn credits toward associate degrees with participating two-year colleges. The degrees are granted in seven fields that relate to seven work specialties in the Navy: data processing, digital electronics; communications electronics; management science; law enforcement; aviation maintenance; and general studies.

• DOES THE U.S. AIR FORCE OFFER ANYTHING SIGNIFICANTLY DIFFERENT?

Yes, but first note that, like the other services, the Air Force will pay 75 percent of the tuition cost of courses that you take at accredited colleges and universities while off-duty. Also, like the Navy's program leading to a two-year college diploma, there is the Community College of the Air Force. Enrollment in CCAF is free, and lots of your Air Force job-related technical training will earn you credits toward graduation. The Navy had eight programs: the Air Force has eighty, including law enforcement, aircraft and missile maintenance, and electronics and telecommunications.

The Air Force also has something called ROTC Airman Scholarship Commissioning Program. It allows enlisted personnel to use two-, three-, or four-year ROTC scholarships to get a degree while in residence at a civilian college and earn a commission, too. Once there, you're just like any other ROTC scholarship student: your tuition and academic fees are paid and you get $100 a month while you're in school. To enter this program, you have to qualify for pilot, navigator, or missile training, or you must pursue one of the specified scientific, engineering, mathematical, or technical degrees. The Army and Navy also have similar programs that allow enlisted members to use ROTC scholarships to pay for college and work toward a commission.

What's unique to the Air Force is the Airman Education and Commissioning Program. This program is for people who already have at least forty-five semester hours of college credit, thirty of them transferable to a scientific technical degree. You attend college full time while drawing the pay and allowances of a staff sergeant, and the Air Force picks up your tuition.

There's one other program, BOOTSTRAP—also for enlisted personnel who are nearly finished with college. Selected participants have up to one year to complete their degrees at civilian schools while receiving full pay and allowances. But you must pay all your own tuition charges and fees. Once you've graduated, you have the opportunity to compete for a slot at the Air Force Officers Training School and for a commission.

• I'VE HEARD THAT THERE ARE NONGOVERNMENT SCHOLARSHIPS AVAILABLE FOR PEOPLE INTERESTED IN A MILITARY CAREER. IS THAT TRUE?

There are scholarships, grants, and loans to help students through college and into the service. But there is also financial aid for students who don't intend to enter the military. This aid comes from veterans and other service-related organizations.

So, strictly speaking, you don't have to be interested in a military career to be eligible for many of these financial aid programs.

Now you know about the options that are available to help pay your child's college bills. In our final chapter, we describe what choices are open to you when it comes to actually forking over the cash.

CHAPTER 14

PAY DAY

Even when you have to pay up, it might not be as bad as writing a check for the full tuition. Check into the school's payment options.

If you're lucky, you're dealing with a college that lets you pay in installments spread over nine and sometimes twelve months. If you are extraordinarily lucky, the college will impose no fee for this service and will charge no interest on the outstanding balance.

This no-fee, no-interest arrangement is the best deal possible in installment plans. Even if you have the money all together, you can keep it in the bank or a money market fund earning interest while paying the school its due one month at a time. (Sometimes, though, schools charge a small enrollment fee to people who want to use an installment plan.)

What might be significant, however, is the interest a school can charge on the unpaid balance you owe. Ask about the rate of interest. If you can borrow the money at a cheaper rate elsewhere—from, say, a credit union or perhaps from your employer, you'd be better off to take the loan and pay the school in a lump sum.

Some schools allow you to pay their tuition and fees by credit card. That's fine if you pay off the balance when the credit card bill comes due. But credit card interest rates are high—as much as 21 percent or more. The monthly interest charges on an unpaid balance of, say, $10,000, can exceed $175. And since credit card interest charges are not deductible at all on your federal income tax, credit card credit should be your last resort in paying college bills.

One last point in the payment department: ask about guaranteed tuition plans at the financial aid office of your child's school. Some schools offer them. These plans simply guarantee that tuition charges won't go up for you while your child is attending the school, regardless of what happens to tuition rates in general. So you'll know exactly how much your tuition charges are going to be over the next four years. This guarantee doesn't extend to other fees and to room and board expenses, but every little bit helps. See Appendix E for a list of schools that do offer these plans.

APPENDICES

SOURCES OF LOANS

There are plenty of borrowing opportunities available to parents and their college-bound youngsters. Here's where to find them.

ALABAMA
Alabama Commission of
Higher Education,
Suite 221, Court Square,
Montgomery   36197–0001

ALASKA
Alaska Commission on
Post-Secondary Education,
Division of
Student Financial Aid,
400 Willoughby Ave., Box FP,
Juneau   99811

ARIZONA
Arizona Educational Loan
Program,
200 North Central Ave.,
Suite 621,
Phoenix   85004

ARKANSAS
Arkansas Student Loan
Guarantee Foundation,
219 South Victory,
Little Rock   72201

CALIFORNIA
California Student Aid
Commission,
1410 5th St.,
Sacramento   95814

COLORADO
Colorado Student Loan
Program,
Suite 500, 11990 Grant,
North Glen   80233

CONNECTICUT
Connecticut Department of
Higher Education,
61 Woodland St.,
Hartford   06105

Connecticut Loan Program,
25 Pratt St.,
Hartford   06103

DELAWARE
Delaware Post-Secondary
Education Commission,
820 French St.,
Wilmington   19801

DISTRICT OF COLUMBIA
District of Columbia,
Higher Loan Program,
Suite 1000,
1023 15th Street N.W.
Washington   20005

District of Columbia,
Office of
Post-Secondary Education,
Suite 600, 1331 H. Street N.W.
Washington   20005

FLORIDA
Florida Department of
Education,
Office of Student
Financial Assistance,
The Capitol,
Tallahassee   32399

GEORGIA
Georgia Student Finance
Authority,
Suite 200,
2082 East Exchange Place,
Tucker   30084

HAWAII
Hawaii Educational Loan
Program,
P.O. Box 22187,
Honolulu   96822

IDAHO
Idaho State Board of
Education,
Room 307,
650 West State St.,
Boise   83720

Student Loan Fund of Idaho,
Processing Center,
P.O. Box 730,
Fruitland   83619

ILLINOIS
Illinois State Scholarship
Commission,
106 Wilmont Road,
Deerfield   60015

INDIANA
Indiana Student Assistance
Commission,
1st Floor,
964 North Pennsylvania Ave.,
Indianapolis   46204

IOWA
Iowa College Aid Commission,
201 Jewett Building,
9th and Grand,
Des Moines   50309

KANSAS
Kansas Board of
Regents,
Suite 609,
Capitol Tower,
Topeka   66603

Kansas Higher Education
Assistance Foundation,
Suite 600,
6800 College Blvd.,
Overland Park   66211

KENTUCKY
Kentucky Higher Education
Assistance Authority,
1050 U.S. 127 South,
Frankfort   40601

LOUISIANA
Louisiana Governor's
Commission on Education
Services, Loan Division,
P.O. Box 44127,
Capitol Station,
Baton Rouge   70804

MAINE
Maine Department of
Educational and Cultural
Services,
State House Station 119,
Augusta   04333

MARYLAND
Maryland Higher Education
Loan Corporation,
Room 305,
2100 Guilford Ave.,
Baltimore   21218

Maryland State Scholarship
Administration,
Room 207,
2100 Guilford Ave.,
Baltimore   21218

MASSACHUSETTS
Massachusetts Board of
Regents of Higher Education,
Room 600, 150 Causeway St.,
Boston   02114

Massachusetts Higher
Education Assistance
Corporation,
Berkeley Place, 330 Stuart St.,
Boston   02116

MICHIGAN
Michigan Department of
Education,
Student Financial Assistance
Services,
P.O. Box 3008
Lansing   48909

MINNESOTA
Minnesota Higher Education
Assistance Foundation,
Suite 500, 85 East 7th St.,
St. Paul   55101

Minnesota Higher Education
Coordinating Board,
Suite 400, Capitol Square,
550 Cedar St.,
St. Paul   55101

MISSISSIPPI
Mississippi Guaranteed
Student Loan Agency,
P.O. Box 342,
Jackson   39205

Mississippi Post-Secondary
Education Financial Assistance
Board,
P.O. Box 2336,
Jackson   39225

MISSOURI
Missouri Coordinating Board
for Higher Education,
101 Adams St.,
Jefferson City   65101

MONTANA
Montana Guaranteed Student
Loan Program,
33 South Last Chance Gulch,
Helena   59620

NEBRASKA
Nebraska Coordinating
Commission for
Post-Secondary Education,
P.O. Box 95005,
Lincoln   68509

Nebraska Higher Education
Assistance Foundation,
Suite 304,
Cornhusker Bank Building,
Lincoln   68251

NEVADA
Nevada Department of
Education,
400 West King St.,
Capitol Complex,
Carson City   89710

NEW HAMPSHIRE
New Hampshire Higher
Education Assistance
Foundation,
P.O. Box 877,
Concord   03302

New Hampshire
Post-Secondary Education
Commission,
2½ Beacon St.,
Concord   03301

NEW JERSEY
New Jersey Department of
Higher Education,
CN 540,
Trenton   08625

New Jersey Higher Education
Assistance Authority,
CN 543,
Trenton   08625

NEW MEXICO
New Mexico Educational
Assistance Foundation,
P.O. Box 27020,
Albuquerque   87125

NEW YORK
New York State Higher
Education Services
Corporation,
99 Washington Ave.,
Albany   12255

NORTH CAROLINA
North Carolina
State Education
Assistance Authority,
P.O. Box 2688,
Chapel Hill   27515

NORTH DAKOTA
Bank of North Dakota,
Student Loan Division,
P.O. Box 5509,
Bismarck   58502

North Dakota Student
Financial Assistance Program,
10th Floor, State Capitol,
Bismarck   58505

OHIO
Ohio Board of Regents,
Student Assistance Office,
3600 State Office Tower,
30 East Broad St.,
Columbus   43216

Ohio Student Loan
Commission,
P.O. Box 16610,
Columbus   43266

OKLAHOMA
Oklahoma State Regents
for Higher Education,
500 Education Building,
State Capitol Complex,
Oklahoma City   73105

OREGON
Oregon State Scholarship
Commission,
1445 Willamette St.,
Eugene   97401

PENNSYLVANIA
Pennsylvania Higher Education
Assistance Agency,
660 Boas St.,
Harrisburg   17102

RHODE ISLAND
Rhode Island Higher Education
Assistance Authority,
560 Jefferson Blvd.,
Warwick   02886

SOUTH CAROLINA
South Carolina Student Loan
Corporation,
Suite 210, Interstate Center,
Columbia   29221

SOUTH DAKOTA
South Dakota Department
of Education,
700 Governors Dr.,
Pierre   57501

South Dakota Education
Assistance Corporation,
115 1st Ave. S.W.,
Aberdeen   57401

TENNESSEE
Tennessee Student Assistance
Corporation,
Suite 1950, Parkway Towers,
404 James Robertson Parkway,
Nashville   37219

TEXAS
Texas Guaranteed Student
Loan Corporation,
P.O. Box 15996,
Austin   78761

UTAH
Utah Board of Regents,
Suite 550, 3 Triad Center,
355 North Temple,
Salt Lake City   84180

VERMONT
Vermont Student Assistance
Corporation,
P.O. Box 2000,
Winooski   05404

VIRGINIA
Virginia Council of
Higher Education,
101 North 14th St.,
James Monroe Bldg.,
Richmond   23219

Virginia State Education
Assistance Authority,
Suite 300, 6 North 6th St.,
Richmond   23219

WASHINGTON
Washington Higher Education
Coordinating Board,
EW–11, 908 East 5th Ave.,
Olympia 98504

Washington Student Loan
Guaranty Association,
500 Colman Bldg.,
811 1st Ave.,
Seattle   98104

WEST VIRGINIA
West Virginia Board
of Regents,
P.O. Box 4007,
Charleston   25364

West Virginia Higher
Education Assistance
Foundation,
P.O. Box 591,
Charleston   25322

WISCONSIN
Great Lakes Higher Education
Corporation,
2401 International Lane,
Madison   53704

Wisconsin Higher Education
Aid Board,
P.O. Box 7885,
Madison   53707

WYOMING
Wyoming Community College
Commission,
3rd Floor, Barrett Bldg.,
2301 Central Ave.,
Cheyenne   82002

Wyoming Higher Education
Assistance Foundation,
Suite 320, 1912 Capitol Ave.,
Cheyenne   82001

Schools Offering Prepayment Plans

Which colleges and universities offer lower tuition rates to students who pay early? Here's our checklist—arranged alphabetically by state.

ALABAMA
Faulkner University,
Montgomery   36193

ARIZONA
Western International University,
Phoenix   85021

ARKANSAS
John Brown University,
Siloam Springs   72761

Southern Baptist College,
Walnut Ridge   72476

CALIFORNIA
Azusa Pacific University,
Azusa   91702

Christian Heritage College,
El Cajon   92019

Compton Community College,
Compton   90221

National University,
San Diego   92108

Northrop University,
Los Angeles   90045

Pacific Union College,
Angwin   94508

St. Mary's College,
Moraga   94575

Santa Clara University,
Santa Clara   95053

Southern California College,
Costa Mesa   92626

University of Redlands,
Redlands   92373

University of San Diego,
San Diego   92110

University of San Francisco,
San Francisco   94117

University of Southern
California,
Los Angeles   90089

Westmont College,
Santa Barbara   93108

COLORADO
Colorado College,
Colorado Springs   80903

Colorado Technical College,
Colorado Springs   80907

CONNECTICUT
Hartford College for Women,
Hartford   06105

University of Bridgeport,
Bridgeport   06601

Yale University,
New Haven   06520

DISTRICT OF COLUMBIA
Catholic University of America,
Washington   20064

George Washington University,
Washington   20052

Mount Vernon College,
Washington   20007

Southeastern University,
Washington   20024

FLORIDA
Art Institute of
Fort Lauderdale,
Fort Lauderdale   33316

Florida International
University,
Miami   33199

Hobe Sound Bible College,
Hobe Sound   33455

Jacksonville University,
Jacksonville   32211

University of Miami,
Miami   33124

University of South Florida,
Tampa   33620

GEORGIA
Morris Brown College,
Atlanta   30314

Oglethorpe University,
Atlanta   30319

IDAHO
College of Idaho,
Caldwell   83605

ILLINOIS
Barat College,
Lake Forest   60045

Columbia College,
Chicago   60605

Midstate College,
Peoria   61602

National College of Education,
Evanston   60201

Quincy College,
Quincy   62301

Trinity College,
Deerfield   60015

University of Chicago,
Chicago   60637

INDIANA
Anderson University,
Anderson   46012

Butler University,
Indianapolis   46208

DePauw University,
Greencastle   46135

Goshen College,
Goshen   46526

Huntington College,
Huntington   46750

Indiana Wesleyan University,
Marion   46953

Rose-Hulman Institute of
Technology,
Terre Haute   47803

Summit Christian College,
Fort Wayne   46807

IOWA
Coe College,
Cedar Rapids   52402

Cornell College,
Mount Vernon   52314

Grinnell College,
Grinnell   50112

Luther College,
Decorah   52101

Simpson College,
Indianola   50125

Vennard College,
University Park   52595

Westmar College,
Le Mars   51031

KANSAS
Friends Bible College,
Haviland   67059

Hesston College,
Hesston   67062

Kansas Wesleyan,
Salina   67401

Ottawa University,
Ottawa   66067

KENTUCKY
Centre College,
Danville   40422

Kentucky Christian College,
Grayson   41143

MAINE
College of the Atlantic,
Bar Harbor   04653

Husson College,
Bangor   04401

Unity College,
Unity   04988

University of New England,
Biddeford   04005

MARYLAND
Columbia Union College,
Takoma Park   20912

Hood College,
Frederick   21701

Johns Hopkins University,
Baltimore   21218

Loyola College,
Baltimore   21210

Mount St. Mary's College,
Emmitsburg   21727

St. John's College,
Annnapolis   21401

Washington Bible College,
Lanham   20706

Western Maryland College,
Westminster   21157

MASSACHUSETTS
American International
College,
Springfield   01109

Atlantic Union College,
South Lancaster   01561

Bentley College,
Waltham   02154

Boston College,
Chestnut Hill   02167

Clark University,
Worcester   01610

College of the Holy Cross,
Worcester   01610

Elms College,
Chicopee   01013

Gordon College,
Wenham   01984

Harvard University,
Cambridge   02138

Marian Court Junior College,
Swampscott   01907

Merrimack College,
North Andover   01845

Mount Holyoke College,
South Hadley   01075

Pine Manor College,
Chestnut Hill   02167

Regis College,
Weston   02193

Smith College,
Northampton   01063

Tufts University,
Medford   02155

Wellesley College,
Wellesley   02181

Wheaton College,
Norton   02766

MICHIGAN
Alma College,
Alma   48801

Andrews University,
Berrien Springs 49104

Aquinas College,
Grand Rapids 49506

Calvin College,
Grand Rapids 49546

Cleary College,
Ypsilanti 48197

Hope College,
Holland 49423

Olivet College,
Olivet 49076

Spring Arbor College,
Spring Arbor 49283

University of Detroit,
Detroit 48221

MINNESOTA
Bethel College,
St. Paul 55112

Carleton College,
Northfield 55057

College of St. Benedict,
St. Joseph 56374

College of St. Thomas,
St. Paul 55105

Concordia College,
Moorhead 56560

Hamline University,
St. Paul 55104

St. John's University,
Collegeville 56321

St. Olaf College,
Northfield 55057

MISSISSIPPI
Millsaps College,
Jackson 39210

Tougaloo College,
Tougaloo 39174

Wood Junior College,
Mathiston 39752

MISSOURI
Avila College,
Kansas City 64145

Central Bible College,
Springfield 65803

Drury College,
Springfield 65802

Northeast Missouri State
University,
Kirksville 63501

Northwest Missouri
State University,
Maryville 64468

Tarkio College,
Tarkio 64491

University of Missouri,
Columbia 65211

Washington University,
St. Louis 63130

William Jewell College,
Liberty 64068

NEBRASKA
Creighton University,
Omaha   68178

Union College,
Lincoln   68506

University of Nebraska,
Omaha   68182

NEW HAMPSHIRE
Dartmouth College,
Hanover   03755

Franklin Pierce College,
Rindge   03461

NEW JERSEY
Berkeley School of
Garret Mount,
West Paterson   07424

Drew University,
Madison   07940

Northeastern Bible College,
Essex Falls   07021

Seton Hall University,
South Orange   07079

NEW YORK
Alfred University,
Alfred   14802

Barnard College,
New York   10027

Canisius College,
Buffalo   14208

Colgate University,
Hamilton   13346

College of New Rochelle,
New Rochelle   10805

Columbia University,
New York   10027

Cornell University,
Ithaca   14853

D'Youville College,
Buffalo   14201

Fordham University,
Bronx   10458

Hobart College,
Geneva   14456

Keuka College,
Keuka Park   14478

Marist College,
Poughkeepsie   12601

New York University,
New York   10003

Nyack College,
Nyack   10960

Rochester Institute
of Technology,
Rochester   14623

Skidmore College,
Saratoga Springs   12866

Syracuse University,
Syracuse   13244

University of Rochester,
Rochester   14627

William Smith College,
Geneva   14456

NORTH CAROLINA
Duke University,
Durham   27706

Louisburg College,
Louisburg   27549

Methodist College,
Fayetteville   28311

NORTH DAKOTA
Jamestown College,
Jamestown   58401

OHIO
Case Western Reserve
University,
Cleveland   44106

Cedarville College,
Cedarville   45314

Cincinnati Bible College
and Seminary,
Cincinnati   45204

Circleville Bible College,
Circleville   43113

Hiram College,
Hiram   44234

Kenyon College,
Gambier   43022

Lake Erie College,
Painesville   44077

Malone College,
Canton   44709

Marietta College,
Marietta   45750

Mount Union College,
Alliance   44601

Ohio Northern University,
Ada   45810

Ohio Wesleyan University,
Delaware   43015

Rio Grande College,
Rio Grande   45674

Union Institute,
Cincinnati   45202

OKLAHOMA
Oklahoma Christian College,
Oklahoma City   73136

Southern Nazarene University,
Bethany   73008

OREGON
Linfield College,
McMinnville   97128

Pacific University,
Forest Grove   97116

PENNSYLVANIA
Academy of the New Church,
Bryn Athyn   19009

Allegheny College,
Meadville   16335

Bryn Mawr College,
Bryn Mawr   19010

Duquesne University,
Pittsburgh   15282

Geneva College,
Beaver Falls   15010

Gettysburg College,
Gettysburg   17325

Lafayette College,
Easton   18042

Lancaster Bible College,
Lancaster   17601

Mercyhurst College,
Erie   16546

Spring Garden College,
Philadelphia   19119

University of Pennsylvania,
Philadelphia   19104

SOUTH CAROLINA
Presbyterian College,
Clinton   29325

TENNESSEE
Milligan College,
Milligan   37682

Southern College of
Seventh-Day Adventists,
Collegedale   37315

Tusculum College,
Greeneville   37743

Vanderbilt University,
Nashville   37240

TEXAS
Huston-Tillotson College,
Austin   78702

Lon Morris College,
Jacksonville   75766

St. Mary's University,
San Antonio   78228

Schreiner College,
Kerrville   78028

Southern Methodist University,
Dallas   75275

Southwestern Adventist
College,
Keene   76059

Southwestern Assemblies of
God College,
Waxahachie   75165

Trinity University,
San Antonio   78212

Wayland Baptist University,
Plainview   79072

VERMONT
Norwich University,
Northfield   05663

Southern Vermont College,
Bennington   05201

VIRGINIA
Liberty University,
Lynchburg   24506

Lynchburg College,
Lynchburg   24501

Marymount University,
Arlington   22207

WASHINGTON
Griffin College,
Seattle   98121

Pacific Lutheran University,
Tacoma   98447

Seattle University,
Seattle   98122

Walla Walla College,
College Place   99324

WEST VIRGINIA
Bethany College,
Bethany   26032

WISCONSIN
Lakeland College,
Sheboygan   53082

Marquette University,
Milwaukee   53233

Northland College,
Ashland   54806

APPENDIX C

SCHOOLS OFFERING COOPERATIVE EDUCATION PROGRAMS

Cooperative education programs, which combine academic study with on-the-job experience and training in a field of a student's choosing, are becoming increasingly popular.

Here's where to find them.

ALABAMA

Alabama State University, Montgomery 36195

Auburn University, Auburn 36849

Auburn University, Montgomery 39193

Brewer State Junior College, Fayette 35555

Huntington College, Montgomery 36194

Jacksonville State University, Jacksonville 36265

John C. Calhoun State College, Decatur 35609

Lurleen B. Wallace State Junior College, Andalusia 36420

Samford University, Birmingham 35229

Tuskegee University, Tuskegee 36088

University of Alabama, Birmingham 35294

University of Alabama,
Huntsville   35899

University of Alabama,
Tuscaloosa   35487

University of Montevallo,
Montevallo   35115

University of South Alabama,
Mobile   36688

ALASKA
University of Alaska,
Juneau   99801

ARIZONA
Arizona Western College,
Yuma   85366

Cochise College,
Douglas   85607

Glendale Community College,
Glendale   85302

Mohave Community College,
Kingman   86401

Northern Arizona University,
Flagstaff   86011

Pima Community College,
Tucson   85702

Scottsdale Community College,
Scottsdale   85256

University of Arizona,
Tucson   85721

ARKANSAS
Arkansas College,
Batesville   72503

Harding University,
Searcy   72143

Mississippi County Community
College,
Blytheville   72316

North Arkansas Community
College,
Harrison   72601

University of Arkansas,
Fayetteville   72701

Westark Community College,
Fort Smith   72913

CALIFORNIA
American River College,
Sacramento   95841

Bakersfield College,
Bakersfield   93305

California College of Arts and
Crafts,
Oakland   94618

California Polytechnic State
University,
San Luis Obispo   93407

California State University,
Bakersfield   93311

California State Polytechnic
University,
Pomona   91768

California State University,
Dominguez Hills   90747

California State University,
Fresno   93740

California State University,
Hayward   94542

California State University,
Long Beach   80840

California State University,
Los Angeles   90032

California State University,
Northridge   91330

California State University,
Sacramento   95819

Canada Community College,
Redwood City   94061

Chabot College,
Hayward   94545

Chapman College,
Orange   92666

College of Notre Dame,
Belmont   94002

College of San Mateo,
San Mateo   94402

College of the Sequoias,
Vialia   93277

College of the Siskiyous,
Weed   96094

Contra Costa College,
San Pablo   94806

De Anza College,
Cupertino   95104

East Los Angeles College,
Monterey Park   91754

Evergreen Valley College,
San Jose   95135

Foothill College,
Los Altos Hills   94022

Fresno City College,
Fresno   93741

Golden Gate University,
San Francisco   94105

Grossmont College,
El Cajon   92020

Humboldt State University,
Arcata   95521

Kings River Community
College,
Reedley   93654

Laney College,
Oakland   94607

Long Beach City College,
Long Beach   90808

Los Angeles City College,
Los Angeles   90029

Los Angeles Pierce College,
Woodland Hills   91371

Los Angeles Trade-Tech
College,
Los Angeles   90015

Los Angeles Valley College,
Van Nuys   91401

Los Medanos College,
Pittsburg   94565

Merced College,
Merced   95348

Merritt College,
Oakland   94619

Monterey Peninsula College,
Monterey   93940

Ohlone College,
Fremont   94539

Palomar College,
San Marcos   92069

Riverside City College,
Riverside   92506

Sacramento City College,
Sacramento   95822

San Bernadino Valley College,
San Bernadino   92410

San Diego State University,
San Diego   92182

San Jose State University,
San Jose   95192

Santa Ana College,
Santa Ana   92706

Santa Clara University,
Santa Clara   95053

Santa Rosa Junior College,
Santa Rosa   95401

Skyline College,
San Bruno   94066

Solano Community College,
Suisun City   94585

Southwestern College,
Chula Vista   92010

University of California,
Berkeley   94720

University of California,
Los Angeles   90024

University of California,
Riverside   92521

University of the Pacific,
Stockton   95211

Victor Valley College,
Victorville   92392

West Los Angeles College,
Culver City   90230

COLORADO
Aims Community College,
Greeley   80632

Arapahoe Community College,
Littleton   80160

Colorado School of Mines,
Golden   80401

Colorado State University,
Fort Collins   80523

Colorado Technical College,
Colorado Springs   80907

Fort Lewis College,
Durango   81301

Front Range Community
College,
Westminster   80030

Mesa College,
Grand Junction   81502

Metropolitan State College,
Denver   80204

Northeastern Junior College,
Sterling   80751

Pikes Peak Community
College,
Colorado Springs   80906

Red Rocks Community
College,
Lakewood   80401

University of Colorado,
Boulder   80309

University of Colorado,
Denver   80204

University of Denver,
Denver   80208

CONNECTICUT
Central Connecticut State
University,
New Britain   06050

Hartford College for Women,
Hartford   06105

Housatonic Regional
Community College,
Bridgeport   06608

Mattatuck Community
College,
Waterbury   06706

Sacred Heart University,
Bridgeport   06432

Southern Connecticut State
University,
New Haven   06515

University of Bridgeport,
Bridgeport   06601

University of Connecticut,
Storrs   06269

University of Hartford,
West Hartford   06117

University of New Haven,
West Haven   06516

Western Connecticut State
University,
Danbury   06810

DELAWARE
Delaware Technical and
Community College,
Georgetown   19947

Goldey Beacom College,
Wilmington   19408

University of Delaware,
Newark   19716

Wesley College,
Dover   19901

DISTRICT OF COLUMBIA
American University,
Washington   20016

Gallaudet University,
Washington   20002

George Washington University,
Washington   20052

Strayer College,
Washington   20005

University of the District of
Columbia,
Washington   20008

FLORIDA
Bethune-Cookman College,
Daytona Beach   32115

Brevard Community College,
Cocoa   32922

Broward Community College,
Fort Lauderdale   33301

Central Florida Community
College,
Ocala   32678

Embry-Riddle Aeronautical
University,
Daytona   32114

Florida Atlantic University,
Boca Raton   33431

Florida Institute of Technology,
Melbourne   32901

Florida International
University,
Miami   33199

Florida State University,
Tallahassee   32306

Gulf Coast Community
College,
Panama City   32401

Lake Sumter Community
College,
Leesburg   34788

Manatee Community College,
Bradenton   34207

Miami-Dade Community
College,
Miami   33132

Nova University,
Fort Lauderdale   33314

Okaloosa-Walton Junior
College,
Niceville   32578

St. Thomas University,
Miami   33054

Sante Fe Community College,
Gainesville   32602

Seminole Community College,
Sanford   32773

University of Central Florida,
Orlando   32816

University of Florida,
Gainesville   32611

University of Miami,
Coral Gables   33124

University of North Florida,
Jacksonville   32216

University of South Florida,
Tampa   33620

University of West Florida,
Pensacola   32514

Valencia Community College,
Orlando   32802

GEORGIA
Albany State College,
Albany   31705

Atlanta University,
Atlanta   30314

Augusta College,
Augusta   30910

Berry College,
Rome   30149

DeVry Institute of Technology,
Decatur   30030

Georgia College,
Milledgeville   31061

Georgia Institute of
Technology,
Atlanta   30332

Georgia Southern University,
Statesboro   30460

Georgia Southwestern College,
Americus   31709

Georgia State University,
Atlanta   30303

Kennesaw College,
Marietta   30061

Middle Georgia College,
Cochran   31014

Morehouse College,
Atlanta   30314

Savannah State College,
Savannah   31404

University of Georgia,
Athens   30602

Valdosta State College,
Valdosta   31698

West Georgia College,
Carrollton   30118

HAWAII
Brigham Young University,
Laie   96762

Hawaii Community College,
Hilo   96720

Hawaii Pacific University,
Honolulu   96813

Honolulu Community College,
Honolulu   96817

Maui Community College,
Kahului   96732

University of Hawaii,
Honolulu   96822

IDAHO
University of Idaho,
Moscow   83843

ILLINOIS
Bradley University,
Peoria   61625

Chicago State University,
Chicago   60628

Columbia College,
Chicago   60605

DeVry Institute of Technology,
Chicago   60618

DeVry Institute of Technology,
Lombard   60148

Elmhurst College,
Elmhurst   60126

Illinois Institute of Technology,
Chicago   60616

Illinois State University,
Normal   61761

Northern Illinois University,
De Kalb   60115

Sangamon State University,
Springfield   62794

School of the Art Institute of
Chicago,
Chicago   60603

Southern Illinois University,
Carbondale   62901

Southern Illinois University,
Edwardsville   62026

Triton College,
River Grove   60171

Truman College,
Chicago   60640

University of Illinois,
Chicago   60680

University of Illinois at Urbana-
Champaign,
Urbana   61801

Wright College,
Chicago   60634

INDIANA
Calumet College,
Whiting   46394

Indiana Institute of
Technology,
Fort Wayne   46803

Indiana State University,
Terre Haute   47809

Indiana University,
Bloomington   47405

Indiana University Southeast,
New Albany   47150

Tri-State University,
Angola   46703

University of Evansville,
Evansville   47722

University of Southern Indiana,
Evansville   47712

Valparaiso University,
Valparaiso   46383

IOWA
Clarke College,
Dubuque   52001

Clinton Community College,
Clinton   52732

Des Moines Area Community
College,
Ankeny   50021

Drake University,
Des Moines   50311

Indian Hills Community
College,
Ottumwa   52501

Iowa State University,
Ames   50011

Marycrest College,
Davenport   52804

Muscatine Community College,
Muscatine   52761

North Iowa Area Community
College,
Mason City   50401

Northwestern College,
Orange City   51041

St. Ambrose University,
Davenport   52803

University of Iowa,
Iowa City   52242

University of Northern Iowa,
Cedar Falls   50614

KANSAS
Benedictine College,
Atchison   66002

Bethany College,
Lindsborg   67456

Cowley County Community
College,
Arkansas City   67005

Donnelly College,
Kansas City   66102

Emporia State University,
Emporia   66801

Garden City Community
College,
Garden City   67846

Hesston College,
Hesston   67062

Johnson County Community
College,
Overland Park   66210

Kansas Newman College,
Wichita   67213

Kansas State University,
Manhattan   66506

Labette Community College,
Parsons   67357

Pittsburg State University,
Pittsburg   66762

Wichita State University,
Wichita   67208

KENTUCKY
Eastern Kentucky University,
Richmond   40475

Hazard Community College,
Hazard   41701

Jefferson Community College,
Louisville   40202

Kentucky State University,
Frankfort   40601

Murray State University,
Murray   42071

Northern Kentucky University,
Highland Heights   41076

Somerset Community College,
Somerset   42501

Thomas More College,
Crestview   41017

University of Kentucky,
Lexington   40506

University of Louisville,
Louisville   40292

Western Kentucky University,
Bowling Green   42101

LOUISIANA
Louisiana Technical University,
Ruston   71272

Southeastern Louisiana
University,
Hammond   70402

University of New Orleans,
New Orleans   70148

MAINE
College of the Atlantic,
Bar Harbor   04653

Husson College,
Bangor   04401

Unity College,
Unity   04988

University of Maine,
Augusta   04330

University of Maine,
Machias   04654

University of Maine,
Orono   04469

MARYLAND
Anne Arundel Community
College,
Arnold   21012

Bowie State University,
Bowie   20715

Columbia Union College,
Takoma Park   20912

Coppin State College,
Baltimore   21216

Frederick Community College.
Frederick   21701

Harford Community College,
Bel Air   21014

Howard Community College,
Columbia   21044

Morgan State University,
Baltimore   21239

Mount St. Mary's College,
Emmitsburg   21727

Prince George's Community
College,
Largo   20772

Towson State University,
Baltimore   21204

University of Maryland,
College Park   20742

University of Maryland,
Princess Anne   21853

MASSACHUSETTS
Boston University,
Boston   02215

Cape Cod Community College,
West Barnstable   02668

Dean Junior College,
Franklin   02038

Gordon College,
Wenham   01984

Holyoke Community College,
Holyoke   01040

Massachusetts Institute of
Technology,
Cambridge   02139

Merrimack College,
North Andover   01845

Middlesex Community College,
Bedford   01730

Mount Wachusett Community
College,
Gardner   01440

Northeastern University,
Boston   02115

North Essex Community
College,
Haverhill   01830

North Shore Community
College,
Beverly   01905

Quinsigamond Community
College,
Worcester   01606

Salem State College,
Salem   01970

Springfield Technical
Community College,
Springfield   01105

Suffolk University,
Boston   02108

University of Lowell,
Lowell   01854

University of Massachusetts,
Amherst   01003

University of Massachusetts,
Boston   02125

Wentworth Institute of
Technology,
Boston   02115

Worcester Polytechnic Institute,
Worcester   01609

MICHIGAN
Albion College,
Albion   49224

Alpena Community College,
Alpena   49707

Bay De Noc Community
College,
Escanaba   49829

Central Michigan University,
Mount Pleasant   48859

Davenport College of Business,
Grand Rapids   49503

Delta College,
University Center   48710

Detroit College of Business,
Dearborn   48126

Eastern Michigan University,
Ypsilanti   48197

Ferris State College,
Big Rapids   49307

GMI Engineering and
Management Institute,
Flint   48504

Grand Valley State University,
Allendale   49401

Henry Ford Community
College,
Dearborn   48128

Kalamazoo College,
Kalamazoo   49007

Kalamazoo Community
College,
Kalamazoo   49009

Kellogg Community College,
Battle Creek   49017

Lake Michigan College,
Benton Harbor   49022

Lawrence Institute of
Technology,
Southfield   48075

Macomb Community College,
Warren   48093

Madonna College,
Livonia   48150

Marygrove College,
Detroit   48221

Mercy College of
Detroit   48219

Michigan Technological
University,
Houghton   49931

Muskegon Community
College,
Muskegon   49442

Northwestern Michigan
College,
Traverse City   49684

Oakland University,
Rochester   48309

Olivet College,
Olivet   49076

Saginaw Valley State
University,
University Center   48710

St. Clair County Community
College,
Port Huron   48061

Schoolcraft College,
Livonia   48152

Siena Heights College,
Adrian   49221

Southwestern Michigan
College,
Dowagiac   49047

University of Detroit,
Detroit   48221

University of Michigan,
Ann Arbor   48109

University of Michigan,
Dearborn   48128

University of Michigan,
Flint   48502

Washtenaw Community
College,
Ann Arbor   48106

Wayne County Community
College,
Detroit   48226

Western Michigan University,
Kalamazoo   49008

MINNESOTA
Anoka-Ramsey Community
College,
Coon Rapids   55433

Augsburg College,
Minneapolis   55454

Bemidji State University,
Bemidji   56601

College of St. Thomas,
St. Paul   55105

Concordia College,
Moorhead   56560

Gustavus Adolphus College,
St. Peter   56082

Mankato State University,
Mankato   56001

Metropolitan State University,
St. Paul   55101

Moorhead State University,
Moorhead   56560

Normandale Community
College,
Bloomington   55431

St. Cloud State University,
St. Cloud   56301

Southwest State University,
Marshall   56258

University of Minnesota,
Crookston   56716

University of Minnesota,
Minneapolis   55455

Willmar Community College,
Willmar   56201

Winona State University,
Winona   55987

MISSISSIPPI
Alcorn State University,
Lorman   39096

Hinds Junior College,
Raymond   39154

Jackson State University,
Jackson   39217

Mississippi College,
Clinton   39058

Mississippi State University,
Mississippi State   39762

Northeast Mississippi Junior
College,
Booneville   38829

Tougaloo College,
Tougaloo   39174

University of Mississippi,
University   38677

MISSOURI
Central Missouri State
University,
Warrensburg 64093

Fontbonne College,
St. Louis 63105

Lincoln University,
Jefferson City 65101

Lindenwood College,
St. Charles 63301

Maryville College,
St. Louis 63141

Missouri Valley College,
Marshall 65340

Northeast Missouri State
University,
Kirksville 63501

Penn Valley Community
College,
Kansas City 64111

Rockhurst College,
Kansas City 64110

St. Louis Community College,
St. Louis 63135

Southwest Missouri State
University
Springfield 65804

University of Missouri,
Columbia 65211

University of Missouri,
Rolla 65401

University of Missouri,
St. Louis 63121

Washington University,
St. Louis 63130

MONTANA
College of Great Falls,
Great Falls 59405

Montana College of Mineral
Science and Technology,
Butte 59701

Montana State University,
Bozeman 59717

University of Montana,
Missoula 59812

NEBRASKA
Central Community College,
Columbus 68602

Central Community College,
Hastings 68902

Chadron State College,
Chadron 69337

Metropolitan Community
College,
Omaha 68103

Southeast Community College,
Lincoln 68520

University of Nebraska,
Lincoln 68588

University of Nebraska,
Omaha 68182

NEVADA
Clark County Community College,
North Las Vegas   89030

Northern Nevada Community College,
Elko   89801

NEW HAMPSHIRE
New Hampshire College,
Manchester   03104

University of New Hampshire,
Durham   03824

NEW JERSEY
Atlantic Community College,
Mays Landing   08330

Bergen Community College,
Paramus   07652

Brookdale Community College,
Lincroft   07738

Burlington County College,
Pemberton   08068

County College of Morris,
Randolph   07869

Glassboro State College,
Glassboro   08028

Jersey City State College,
Jersey City   07305

Kean College of New Jersey,
Union   07083

Mercer County Community College,
Trenton   08690

Middlesex County College,
Edison   08818

Montclair State College,
Upper Montclair   07043

New Jersey Institute of Technology,
Newark   07102

Ocean County College,
Toms River   08753

Passaic County Community College,
Paterson   07509

Ramapo College of New Jersey,
Mahwah   07430

Rider College,
Lawrenceville   08648

Rutgers/Cook College,
New Brunswick   08903

St. Peter's College,
Jersey City   07308

Salem Community College,
Carneys Point   08069

Seton Hall University,
South Orange   07079

Trenton State College,
Trenton   08650

NEW MEXICO
College of Santa Fe,
Santa Fe   87501

Eastern New Mexico University,
Portales   88130

New Mexico Highlands
University,
Las Vegas   87701

New Mexico Institute of
Mining and Technology,
Socorro   87801

New Mexico State University,
Las Cruces   88003

San Juan College,
Farmington   87401

University of New Mexico,
Albuquerque   87131

NEW YORK
Borough of Manhattan
Community College,
New York   10007

City College of New York,
New York   10031

Clarkson College,
Potsdam   13676

College of Insurance,
New York   10007

Cornell University,
Ithaca   14853

Daemen College,
Amherst   14226

Genesee Community College,
Batavia   14020

Hudson Valley Community
College,
Troy   12180

Keuka College,
Keuka Park   14478

Long Island University,
Southhampton   11968

Manhattan College,
Riverdale   10471

Manhattanville College,
Purchase   10577

Marist College,
Poughkeepsie   12601

Marymount College,
Tarrytown   10591

Monroe Community College,
Rochester   14623

Nassau Community College,
Garden City   11530

National Technical Institute
for the Deaf,
Rochester   14623

New York Institute of
Technology,
Old Westbury   11568

New York University,
New York   10003

Pace University,
New York   10038

Polytechnic Institute of
New York,
Brooklyn   11201

Pratt Institute,
Brooklyn   11205

Rensselaer Polytechnic
Institute,
Troy   12180

Rochester Institute of
Technology,
Rochester   14623

Rockland Community College,
Suffern   10901

SUNY Agriculture and
Technology College,
Alfred   14802

SUNY/College at Brockport,
Brockport   14420

SUNY/College at Buffalo,
Buffalo   14260

SUNY/College at Cortland,
Cortland   13045

SUNY/College at Fredonia,
Fredonia   14063

SUNY/College at New Paltz,
New Paltz   12561

SUNY/College at Plattsburgh,
Plattsburgh   12901

SUNY/College of Technology
at Utica-Rome,
Utica   13504

Syracuse University,
Syracuse   13244

United States Merchant
Marine Academy,
Kings Point   11024

NORTH CAROLINA

Beaufort County Community
College,
Washington   27889

Catawba Valley Technical
College,
Hickory   28602

Central Piedmont Community
College,
Charlotte   28235

College of the Albemarle,
Elizabeth City   27906

Craven Community College,
New Bern   28560

East Carolina University,
Greenville   27858

Elizabeth City State University,
Elizabeth City   27909

Elon College,
Elon   27244

Fayetteville State University,
Fayetteville   28301

Fayetteville Technical Institute,
Fayetteville   28303

Guilford Technical Community
College,
Jamestown   27282

Isothermal Community
College,
Spindale   28160

Lenoir Community College,
Kinston   28502

Meredith College,
Raleigh 27607

Mount Olive College,
Mount Olive 28365

North Carolina A&T
State University,
Greensboro 27411

North Carolina State
University,
Raleigh 27695

North Carolina Wesleyan
College,
Rocky Mount 27804

Pitt Community College,
Greenville 27835

Southeastern Community
College,
Whiteville 28472

University of North Carolina,
Charlotte 28223

University of North Carolina,
Greensboro 27412

Wake Technical College,
Raleigh 27603

Wayne Community College,
Goldsboro 27533

Western Carolina University,
Cullowbee 28723

Western Piedmont Community
College,
Morganton 28655

Wilkes Community College,
Wilkesboro 28697

Winston-Salem State
University,
Winston-Salem 27110

NORTH DAKOTA
Jamestown College,
Jamestown 58401

Mayville State University,
Mayville 58257

North Dakota State University,
Fargo 56105

Valley City State College,
Valley City 58072

OHIO
Antioch University,
Yellow Springs 45387

Baldwin-Wallace College,
Berea 44017

Bowling Green State
University,
Bowling Green 43403

Case Western Reserve
University,
Cleveland 44106

Central State University,
Wilberforce 45384

Cincinnati Technical College,
Cincinnati 45223

Cleveland State University,
Cleveland 44115

Cuyahoga Community College,
Parma   44130

Defiance College,
Defiance   43512

Dyke College,
Cleveland   44115

John Carroll University,
Cleveland   44118

Kent State University,
Kent   44242

Lakeland Community College,
Mentor   44060

Marietta College,
Marietta   45750

Miami University,
Oxford   45046

Mount Union College,
Alliance   44601

Notre Dame College,
Cleveland   44121

Ohio State University,
Columbus   43210

Ohio University,
Athens   45701

Sinclair Community College,
Dayton   45402

Stark Technical College,
Canton   44720

University of Akron,
Akron   44325

University of Cincinnati,
Cincinnati   45221

University of Dayton,
Dayton   45469

Wilberforce University,
Wilberforce   45384

Wilmington College,
Wilmington   45177

Wright State University,
Dayton   45435

OKLAHOMA
Carl Albert Junior College,
Poteau   74953

Oklahoma Baptist University,
Shawnee   74801

Oklahoma City Community
College,
Oklahoma City   73159

Rogers State College,
Claremore   74017

Tulsa Junior College,
Tulsa   74135

OREGON
Chemeketa Community
College,
Salem   97309

Clackamas Community
College,
Oregon City   97045

Clatsop Community College,
Astoria   97103

Eastern Oregon State College,
La Grande 97850

Lane Community College,
Eugene 97405

Linn Benton Community
College,
Albany 97321

Oregon Institute of
Technology,
Klamath Falls 97601

Oregon State University,
Corvallis 97331

Portland Community College,
Portland 97219

Portland State University,
Portland 97207

Rogue Community College,
Grants Pass 97527

Southern Oregon State College,
Ashland 97520

Southwestern Oregon
Community College,
Coos Bay 97420

PENNSYLVANIA
Beaver College,
Glenside 19038

Bloomsburg University,
Bloomsburg 17815

Bucks County
Community College,
Newtown 18940

Carnegie Mellon University,
Pittsburgh 15213

Chesnut Hill College,
Philadelphia 19118

Cheyney University,
Cheyney 19319

Community College of
Allegheny County,
Monroeville 15146

Community College of
Allegheny County,
Pittsburgh 15237

Community College of
Allegheny County,
West Mifflin 15122

Delaware County
Community College,
Media 19063

Delaware Valley College of
Science and Agriculture,
Doylestown 18901

Drexel University,
Philadelphia 19104

Hahnemann University,
Philadelphia 19102

Indiana University of
Pennsylvania,
Indiana 15705

King's College,
Wilkes-Barre 18711

La Salle University,
Philadelphia 19141

Lehigh University,
Bethlehem   18015

Lincoln University,
Lincoln   19352

Lockhaven University,
Lockhaven   17745

Mercyhurst College,
Erie   16546

Messiah College,
Grantham   17027

Millersville University of
Pennsylvania,
Millersville   17551

Peirce Junior College,
Philadelphia   19102

Pennsylvania State University,
University Park   16802

Philadelphia College of
Textiles and Science,
Philadelphia   19144

St. Joseph's University,
Philadelphia   19131

St. Vincent College,
Latrobe   15650

Susquehanna University,
Selinsgrove   17870

Temple University,
Philadelphia   19122

Waynesburg College,
Waynesburg   15370

Westmoreland County
Community College,
Youngwood   15697

Widener College of
Widener University,
Chester   19013

Wilkes University,
Wilkes-Barre   18766

RHODE ISLAND
Johnson & Wales University,
Providence   02903

Rhode Island College,
Providence   02908

Roger Williams College,
Bristol   02809

SOUTH CAROLINA
Benedict College,
Columbia   29204

Clemson University,
Clemson   29634

Florence-Darlington
Technical College,
Florence   29501

Furman University,
Greenville   29613

Lander College,
Greenwood   29649

Midlands Technical College,
Columbia   29202

Morris College,
Sumter   29150

University of South Carolina,
Aiken 29801

University of South Carolina,
Columbia 29208

Winthrop College,
Rock Hill 29733

Wofford College,
Spartanburg 29301

SOUTH DAKOTA
South Dakota School of
Mines and Technology,
Rapid City 57701

South Dakota State University,
Brookings 57007

TENNESSEE
Belmont College,
Nashville 37212

Chattanooga State Technical
Community College,
Chattanooga 37406

Cleveland State
Community College,
Cleveland 37320

Columbia State
Community College,
Columbia 38401

East Tennessee
State University,
Johnson City 37614

Fisk University,
Nashville 37208

Middle Tennessee State
University,
Murfreesboro 37132

Roane State
Community College,
Harriman 37748

Shelby State
Community College,
Memphis 38174

University of Tennessee,
Chattanooga 37403

University of Tennessee,
Knoxville 37996

University of Tennessee,
Martin 38238

TEXAS
Amarillo College,
Amarillo 79178

Brookhaven College,
Farmers Branch 75244

Cedar Valley College,
Lancaster 75134

College of the Mainland,
Texas City 77591

Eastfield College,
Mesquite 75150

East Texas State University,
Commerce 75428

El Centro College,
Dallas 75202

Galveston College,
Galveston 77550

Houston Community College,
Houston 77270

Huston-Tillotson College,
Austin   78702

Lamar University,
Beaumont   77710

Midland College,
Midland   79705

Prairie View A&M University,
Prairie View   77446

Richland College,
Dallas   75243

St. Edwards University,
Austin   78704

St. Mary's University,
San Antonio   78228

Sam Houston State University,
Huntsville   77341

San Antonio College,
San Antonio   78284

Southern Methodist University,
Dallas   75275

South Plains College,
Levelland   79336

Texas A&M University,
College Station   77843

Texas Lutheran College,
Seguin   78155

Texas Southern University,
Houston   77004

Texas State Technical Institute,
Waco   78551

Texas Woman's University,
Denton   76204

University of Houston,
Houston   77002

University of Texas,
Arlington   76019

University of Texas,
Austin   78712

UTAH
Brigham Young University,
Provo   84602

Dixie College,
St. George   84770

University of Utah,
Salt Lake City   84112

Utah State University,
Logan   84322

Weber State College,
Ogden   84408

Westminster College,
Salt Lake City   84105

VERMONT
Lyndon State College,
Lyndonville   05851

Norwich University,
Northfield   05663

University of Vermont,
Burlington   05405

VIRGINIA
Blue Ridge Community
College,
Weyers Cave   24486

Central Virginia Community
College,
Lynchburg 24502

George Mason University,
Fairfax 22030

Germanna Community
College,
Locust Grove 22508

Hampton University,
Hampton 23668

Lord Fairfax Community
College,
Middletown 22645

New River Community
College,
Dublin 24084

Norfolk State University,
Norfolk 23504

Northern Virginia Community
College,
Annandale 22003

Old Dominion University,
Norfolk 23529

Patrick Henry Community
College,
Martinsville 24115

Paul D. Camp Community
College,
Franklin 23851

Piedmont Virginia Community
College,
Charlottesville 22901

Thomas Nelson Community
College,
Hampton 23670

Tidewater Community College,
Portsmouth 23703

Tidewater Community College,
Virginia Beach 23456

University of Virginia
Clinch Valley College,
Wise 24293

Virginia Commonwealth
University,
Richmond 23298

Virginia Polytechnic Institute
and State University,
Blacksburg 24061

Virginia State University,
Petersburg 23803

Virginia Union University,
Richmond 23220

Virginia Western Community
College,
Roanoke 24038

WASHINGTON
Central Washington University,
Ellensburg 98926

Clark College,
Vancouver 98663

Columbia Basin College,
Pasco 99301

Eastern Washington University,
Cheney 99004

Edmonds Community College,
Lynnwood   98036

Everett Community College,
Everett   98201

Evergreen State College,
Olympia   98505

Highline Community College,
Des Moines   98198

Lower Columbia College,
Longview   98632

Pacific Lutheran University,
Tacoma   98447

Seattle Central Community
College,
Seattle   98122

Skagit Valley College,
Mount Vernon   98273

South Puget Sound Community
College,
Olympia   98502

Spokane Community College,
Spokane   99207

Tacoma Community College,
Tacoma   98465

Walla Walla College,
Walla Walla   99362

University of Puget Sound,
Tacoma   98416

University of Washington,
Seattle   98195

Washington State University,
Pullman   99164

Wenatchee Valley College,
Wenatchee   98801

Whatcom Community College,
Bellingham   98226

WEST VIRGINIA
Marshall University,
Huntington   25755

Southern West Virginia
Community College,
Logan   25601

University of Charleston,
Charleston   25304

West Virginia Institute of
Technology,
Montgomery   25136

West Virginia State College,
Institute   25112

West Virginia Wesleyan
College,
Buckhannon   26201

Wheeling College,
Wheeling   26003

WISCONSIN
Marquette University,
Milwaukee   53233

Milwaukee Area
Technical College,
Milwaukee   53233

Moraine Park
Technical Institute,
Fond du Lac   54936

Mount Senario College,
Ladysmith   54848

St. Norbert College,
De Pere   54115

University of Wisconsin,
La Crosse   54601

University of Wisconsin,
Madison   53706

University of Wisconsin,
Menominee   54751

University of Wisconsin,
Milwaukee   53201

University of Wisconsin,
River Falls   54022

University of Wisconsin,
Stevens Point   54481

Waukesha County
Technical College,
Pewaukee   53072

WYOMING
Western Wyoming
Community College,
Rock Springs   82901

SCHOOLS OFFERING ROTC

The Army, Navy, Air Force, and Marines all have Reserve Officer Training Corps (ROTC) programs. But first you have to find a school that has an ROTC unit. Not all do.
Here's our checklist.

AIR FORCE

Adelphi University,
Garden City, NY   11530

Agnes Scott College,
Decatur, GA   30030

Alabama State University,
Montgomery, AL   36195

Allentown College of
St. Francis de Sales,
Center Valley, PA   18034

American University,
Washington, DC   20016

Amherst College,
Amherst, MA   01002

Angelo State University,
San Angelo, TX   76909

Anna Maria College for
Men and Women,
Paxton, MA   01612

Arizona State University,
Tempe, AZ   85287

Ashland University,
Ashland, OH   44805

Assumption College,
Worcester, MA   01615

Auburn University,
Auburn, AL   38849

Augsburg College,
Minneapolis, MN 55454

Baker University,
Baldwin City, KS 66006

Baldwin-Wallace College,
Berea, OH 44017

Baptist College at Charleston,
Charleston, SC 29411

Barry University,
Miami Shores, FL 33161

Baylor University,
Waco, TX 76798

Bellarmine College,
Louisville, KY 40205

Bellevue College,
Bellevue, NE 68005

Belmont Abbey College,
Belmont, NC 28012

Belmont College,
Nashville, TN 37212

Benedict College,
Columbia, SC 29204

Bentley College,
Waltham, MA 02154

Bethel College,
St. Paul, MN 55112

Bethune-Cookman College,
Daytona Beach, FL 32115

Biola University,
La Mirada, CA 90639

Birmingham-Southern College,
Birmingham, AL 35254

Bloomfield College,
Bloomfield, NJ 07003

Bloomsburg University of
Pennsylvania,
Bloomsburg, PA 17815

Boston University,
Boston, MA 02215

Bowie State University,
Bowie, MD 20715

Bowling Green State
University,
Bowling Green, OH 43403

Brigham Young University,
Provo, UT 84602

Bryn Mawr College,
Bryn Mawr, PA 19010

Bucknell University,
Lewisburg, PA 17837

Butler University,
Indianapolis, IN 46208

California Institute of
Technology,
Pasadena, CA 91125

California Lutheran University,
Thousand Oaks, CA 91360

California State University,
Fresno, CA 93740

California State University,
Hayward, CA 94542

California State University,
Long Beach, CA   90840

California State University,
Northridge, CA   91330

California State University,
Sacramento, CA   95819

Capital University,
Columbus, OH   43209

Carlow College,
Pittsburgh, PA   15213

Carnegie Mellon University,
Pittsburgh, PA   15213

Case Western Reserve
University,
Cleveland, OH   44106

Catholic University of America,
Washington, DC   20064

Cedar Crest College,
Allentown, PA   18104

Cedarville College,
Cedarville, OH   45314

Central Connecticut State
University,
New Britain, CT   06050

Central Washington University,
Ellensburg, WA   98926

Centre College,
Danville, KY   40422

Chaminade University of
Honolulu,
Honolulu, HI   96816

Chapman College,
Orange, CA   92666

Chicago State University,
Chicago, IL   60628

Christian Brothers College,
Memphis, TN   38104

The Citadel,
Charleston, SC   29409

City College of the City
University of New York,
New York, NY   10031

Claremont McKenna College,
Claremont, CA   91711

Clark College,
Atlanta, GA   30314

Clarkson University,
Potsdam, NY   13676

Clark University,
Worcester, MA   01610

Clemson University,
Clemson, SC   29634

Cleveland State University,
Cleveland, OH   44115

Cogswell Polytechnical College,
Cupertino, CA   95014

Colby College,
Waterville, ME   04901

Colby-Sawyer College,
New London, NH   03257

College Misericordia,
Dallas, PA   18612

College of Aeronautics,
Flushing, NY   11371

College of Charleston,
Charleston, SC   29424

College of Mount St. Joseph,
Cincinnati, OH   45051

College of Mount St. Vincent,
Riverdale, NY   10471

College of St. Catherine,
St. Paul, MN   55105

College of St. Mary,
Omaha, NE   68124

College of St. Rose,
Albany, NY   12203

College of St. Scholastica,
Duluth, MN   55811

College of St. Thomas,
St. Paul, MN   55105

Colorado State University,
Fort Collins, CO   80523

College of the Holy Cross,
Worcester, MA   01610

Columbia College,
Columbia, SC   29203

Columbia University,
New York, NY   10027

Concordia College,
Moorhead, MN   56560

Concordia College,
St. Paul, MN   55104

Concordia Teachers College,
Seward, NE   68434

Cornell University,
Ithaca, NY   14853

Creighton University,
Omaha, NE   68178

Dallas Baptist University,
Dallas, TX   75211

Daniel Webster College,
Nashua, NH   03063

David Lipscomb University,
Nashville, TN   37204

Davidson College,
Davidson, NC   28036

Deaconess College of Nursing,
St. Louis, MO   63139

Delaware State College,
Dover, DE   19910

Delta State University,
Cleveland, MS   38733

Dowling College,
Oakdale, NY   11769

Drake University,
Des Moines, IA   50311

Drexel University,
Philadelphia, PA   19104

Duke University,
Durham, NC   27706

Duquesne University,
Pittsburgh, PA   15282

East Carolina University,
Greenville, NC   27858

Eastern College,
Saint Davids, PA   19087

Eastern Connecticut State
University,
Willimantic, CT   06226

Eastern Michigan University,
Ypsilanti, MI   48197

East Texas State University,
Commerce, TX   75428

Edgewood College,
Madison, WI   53711

Elmhurst College,
Elmhurst, IL   60126

Elmira College,
Elmira, NY   14901

Embry-Riddle Aeronautical
University,
Daytona Beach, FL   32114

Embry-Riddle Aeronautical
University,
Prescott, AZ   86301

Fairleigh Dickinson University,
Madison, NJ   07940

Fairleigh Dickinson University,
Rutherford, NJ   07070

Fairleigh Dickinson University,
Teaneck, NJ   07666

Fairmont State College,
Fairmont, WV   26554

Fayetteville State University,
Fayetteville, NC   28301

Fisk University,
Nashville, TN   37208

Florida Agricultural and
Mechanical University,
Tallahassee, FL   32307

Florida Atlantic University,
Boca Raton, FL   33431

Florida International
University,
Miami, FL   33199

Florida Southern College,
Lakeland, FL   33801

Franklin University,
Columbus, OH   43215

George Mason University,
Fairfax, VA   22030

Georgetown College,
Georgetown, KY   40324

Georgetown University,
Washington, DC   20047

Georgia Institute of
Technology,
Atlanta, GA   30332

Georgia State University,
Statesboro, GA   30458

Golden Gate University,
San Francisco, CA   94105

Gordon College,
Wenham, MA   01984

Goucher College,
Baltimore, MD   21204

Grand Canyon University,
Phoenix, AZ   85061

Green Mountain College,
Poultney, VT   05764

Greensboro College,
Greensboro, NC   27401

Guilford College,
Greensboro, NC   27410

Hamline University,
St. Paul, MN   55104

Harvard University,
Cambridge, MA   02138

Harvey Mudd College,
Claremont, CA   91711

Hawaii Pacific College,
Honolulu, HI   96813

High Point College,
High Point, NC   27261

Hofstra University,
Hempstead, NY   11550

Holy Names College,
Oakland, CA   94619

Howard University,
Washington, DC   20059

Huntingdon College,
Montgomery, AL   36194

Husson College,
Bangor, ME   04401

Illinois Benedictine College,
Lisle, IL   60532

Illinois Institute of Technology,
Chicago, IL   60616

Indiana State University,
Terre Haute, IN   47809

Indiana University,
Bloomington, IN   47405

Indiana University
South Bend, IN   46634

Indiana University Southeast,
New Albany, IN   47150

Iowa State University of
Science and Technology,
Ames, IA   50011

Jersey City State College,
Jersey City, NJ   07305

John Brown University,
Siloam Springs, AR   72761

Johns Hopkins University,
Baltimore, MD   21218

Johnson C. Smith University,
Charlotte, NC   28216

Johnson State College,
Johnson, VT   05656

Kansas State University,
Manhattan, KS   66506

Kean College of New Jersey,
Union, NJ   07083

Kent State University,
Kent, OH   44242

Kentucky State University
Frankfort, KY   40601

King's College,
Wilkes-Barre, PA   18711

Knoxville College,
Knoxville, TN   37921

Kutztown University of
Pennsylvania,
Kutztown, PA   19530

Lafayette College,
Easton, PA   18042

La Roche College,
Pittsburgh, PA   15237

La Salle University,
Philadelphia, PA   19141

Lawrence Technological
University,
Southfield, MI   48075

Lehigh University,
Bethlehem, PA   18015

Le Moyne College,
Syracuse, NY   13214

Lewis-Clark State College,
Lewiston, ID   83501

Lewis University,
Romeoville, IL   60441

Long Island University,
Brooklyn, NY   11201

Louisiana State University and
Agricultural and Mechanical
College,
Baton Rouge, LA   70803

Louisiana Tech University,
Ruston, LA   71272

Loyola College,
Baltimore, MD   21210

Loyola Marymount University,
Los Angeles, CA   90045

Loyola University,
Chicago, IL   60611

Loyola University,
New Orleans, LA   70118

Lubbock Christian University,
Lubbock, TX   79407

Lyndon State College,
Lyndonville, VT   05851

Macalester College,
St. Paul, MN   55105

Manhattan College,
Riverdale, NY   10471

Marian College,
Indianapolis, IN   46222

Marquette University,
Milwaukee, WI   53233

Maryville College,
St. Louis, MO   63141

Marywood College,
Scranton, PA   18509

Massachusetts Institute of
Technology,
Cambridge, MA   02139

McKendree College,
Lebanon, IL   62254

Memphis State University,
Memphis, TN 38152

Mercy College,
Dobbs Ferry, NY 10522

Meredith College,
Raleigh, NC 27607

Merrimack College,
North Andover, MA 01845

Metropolitan State College,
Denver, CO 80204

Miami University,
Oxford, OH 45056

Michigan State University,
East Lansing, MI 48824

Michigan Technological
University,
Houghton, MI 49931

Mid-America Nazarene
College,
Olathe, KS 66061

Middle Tennessee State
University,
Murfreesboro, TN 37132

Mills College,
Oakland, CA 94613

Milwaukee School of
Engineering,
Milwaukee, WI 53201

Mississippi State University,
Mississippi State, MS 39762

Mississippi University for
Women,
Columbus, MS 39701

Molloy College,
Rockville Centre, NY 11570

Monmouth College,
West Long Branch, NJ 07764

Montana State University,
Bozeman, MT 59717

Montclair State College,
Upper Montclair, NJ 07043

Moorhead State University,
Moorhead, MN 56560

Moravian College,
Bethlehem, PA 18018

Morehouse College,
Atlanta, GA 30314

Morris Brown College,
Atlanta, GA 30314

Mount Holyoke College,
South Hadley, MA 01075

Mount St. Mary's College,
Los Angeles, CA 90049

Mount Union College,
Alliance, OH 44601

Muhlenberg College,
Allentown, PA 18104

National University,
San Diego, CA 92108

Nazareth College,
Rochester, NY 14610

Nebraska Wesleyan University,
Lincoln, NE 68504

New England College,
Henniker, NH   03242

New Hampshire College,
Manchester, NH   03104

New Jersey Institute of
Technology,
Newark, NJ   07102

New Mexico State University,
Las Cruces, NM   88003

New York Institute of
Technology,
Old Westbury, NY   11568

New York University,
New York, NY   10011

North Carolina Agricultural
and Technical State University,
Greensboro, NC   27411

North Carolina Central
University,
Durham, NC   27707

North Carolina State
University,
Raleigh, NC   27695

North Central College,
Naperville, IL   60566

North Dakota State University,
Fargo, ND   58105

Northeastern Illinois
University,
Chicago, IL   60625

Northeastern University,
Boston, MA   02115

Northern Arizona University,
Flagstaff, AZ   86011

Northern Kentucky University,
Highland Heights, KY   41076

North Park College,
Chicago, IL   60625

Northrop University,
Los Angeles, CA   90045

Northwestern College,
St. Paul, MN   55113

Northwestern University,
Evanston, IL   60208

Northwood Institute,
Midland, MI   48640

Norwich University,
Northfield, VT   05663

Notre Dame College,
Manchester, NH   03104

Occidental College,
Los Angeles, CA   90041

Oglethorpe University
Atlanta, GA   30319

Ohio Dominican College,
Columbus, OH   43219

Ohio State University,
Columbus, OH   43210

Ohio State University,
Lima, OH   45804

Ohio State University,
Mansfield, OH   44906

Ohio State University,
Marion, OH   43302

Ohio State University,
Newark, OH   43055

Ohio University,
Athens, OH   45701

Ohio University,
Chillicothe, OH   45601

Ohio University,
Lancaster, OH   43130

Ohio Wesleyan University,
Delaware, OH   43015

Oklahoma Christian College,
Oklahoma City, OK   73136

Oklahoma City University,
Oklahoma City, OK   73106

Oklahoma State University,
Stillwater, OK   74078

Oregon State University,
Corvallis, OR   97331

Otterbein College,
Westerville, OH   43081

Our Lady of Holy Cross
College,
New Orleans, LA   70131

Pace University,
Briarcliff, NY   10570

Pace University,
New York, NY   10038

Pace University,
White Plains, NY   10603

Pembroke State University,
Pembroke, NC   28372

Pennsylvania State University,
University Park, PA   16802

Pepperdine University,
Malibu, CA   90265

Plymouth State College,
Plymouth, NH   03264

Point Loma Nazarene College,
San Diego, CA   92106

Point Park College,
Pittsburgh, PA   15222

Polytechnic University,
Brooklyn, NY   11201

Polytechnic University,
Farmingdale, NY   11735

Pomona College,
Claremont, CA   91711

Portland State University,
Portland, OR   97207

Princeton University,
Princeton, NJ   08544

Purdue University,
West Lafayette, IN   47907

Queens College,
Charlotte, NC   28274

Quinnipiac College,
Hamden, CT   06518

Regis College,
Denver, CO   80221

Rensselaer Polytechnic
Institute,
Troy, NY   12180

Rider College,
Lawrenceville, NJ   08648

Roberts Wesleyan College,
Rochester, NY   14624

Rochester Institute of
Technology,
Rochester, NY   14623

Rose-Hulman Institute of
Technology,
Terre Haute, IN   47803

Russell Sage College,
Troy, NY   12180

Rutgers,
New Brunswick, NJ   08903

St. Anselm College,
Manchester, NH   03102

St. Augustine's College,
Raleigh, NC   27610

St. Francis College,
Brooklyn Heights, NY   11201

St. John Fisher College,
Rochester, NY   14618

St. John's University,
Jamaica, NY   11439

St. Joseph's University,
Philadelphia, PA   19131

St. Lawrence University,
Canton, NY   13617

St. Louis College of Pharmacy,
St. Louis, MO   63110

St. Louis University,
St. Louis, MO   63103

St. Mary's College,
Notre Dame, IN   46556

St. Peter's College,
Jersey City, NJ   07306

St. Thomas Aquinas College,
Sparkill, NY   10976

St. Thomas University,
Miami, FL   33054

St. Vincent College,
Latrobe, PA   15650

St. Xavier College,
Chicago, IL   60655

Samford University,
Birmingham, AL   35229

San Diego State University,
San Diego, CA   92182

San Francisco State University,
San Francisco, CA   94132

San Jose State University,
San Jose, CA   95192

Santa Clara University,
Santa Clara, CA   95053

Scripps College,
Claremont, CA   91711

Seattle Pacific University,
Seattle, WA   98119

Seattle University,
Seattle, WA   98122

Seton Hall University,
South Orange, NJ   07079

Shepherd College,
Shepherdstown, WV   25443

Siena College,
Loudonville, NY   12211

Skidmore College,
Saratoga Springs, NY   12866

Smith College,
Northampton, MA   01063

South Dakota State University,
Brookings, SD   57007

Southeast Missouri State
University,
Cape Girardeau, MO   63701

Southern College of
Technology,
Marietta, GA   30060

Southern Connecticut State
University,
New Haven, CT   06515

Southern Illinois University,
Carbondale, IL   62901

Southern Illinois University,
Edwardsville, IL   62026

Southern Methodist University,
Dallas, TX   75275

Spalding University,
Louisville, KY   40203

Spelman College,
Atlanta, GA   30314

Springfield College,
Springfield, MA   01109

Stanford University,
Stanford, CA   94305

SUNY/College at Albany,
Albany, NY   12222

SUNY/College at Binghamton,
Binghamton, NY   13902

SUNY/College at Brockport,
Brockport, NY   14420

SUNY/College at Cortland,
Cortland, NY   13045

SUNY/College at Geneseo,
Geneseo, NY   14454

SUNY/College at Potsdam,
Potsdam, NY   13676

SUNY Maritime College,
Throgs Neck, NY   10465

Stephens College,
Columbia, MO   65215

Stevens Institute of
Technology,
Hoboken, NJ   07030

Syracuse University,
Syracuse, NY   13244

Taylor University,
Upland, IN   46989

Temple University,
Philadelphia, PA   19122

Tennessee State University,
Nashville, TN   37209

Texas A&M University,
College Station, TX   77843

Texas Christian University,
Fort Worth, TX   76129

Texas Lutheran College,
Seguin, TX   78155

Texas Tech University,
Lubbock, TX   79409

Texas Wesleyan University,
Fort Worth, TX   76105

Texas Woman's University,
Denton, TX   76204

Thomas More College,
Crestview Hills, KY   41017

Towson State University,
Towson, MD   21204

Transylvania University,
Lexington, KY   40508

Trenton State College,
Trenton, NJ   08650

Trinity College,
Burlington, VT   05401

Trinity College,
Hartford, CT   06106

Trinity College,
Washington, DC   20017

Trinity University,
San Antonio, TX   78212

Troy State University,
Troy, AL   36082

Tufts University,
Medford, MA   02155

Tulane University,
New Orleans, LA   70118

Tuskegee University,
Tuskegee, AL   36088

Union College,
Schenectady, NY   12308

University of Akron,
Akron, OH   44325

University of Alabama,
Tuscaloosa, AL   35487

University of Arizona,
Tucson, AZ   85721

University of California,
Berkeley, CA   94720

University of California,
Irvine, CA   92717

University of California,
Los Angeles, CA   90024

University of California,
Riverside, CA   92521

University of California,
San Diego, CA   92093

University of Central Florida,
Orlando, FL   32816

University of Chicago,
Chicago, IL   60637

University of Cincinnati,
Cincinnati, OH   45221

University of Colorado,
Boulder, CO   80309

University of Colorado,
Denver, CO   80204

University of Connecticut,
Storrs, CT   06269

University of Dallas,
Irving, TX   75062

University of Dayton,
Dayton, OH   45469

University of Delaware,
Newark, DE   19716

University of the District of
Columbia,
Washington, DC   20008

University of Findlay,
Findlay, OH   45840

University of Florida,
Gainesville, FL   32611

University of Georgia,
Athens, GA   30602

University of Hartford,
West Hartford, CT   06117

University of Hawaii,
Manoa, HI   96822

University of Idaho,
Moscow, ID   83843

University of Illinois,
Chicago, IL   60680

University of Illinois,
Urbana-Champaign,
IL   61801

University of Iowa,
Iowa City, IA   52242

University of Kansas,
Lawrence, KS   66045

University of Kentucky,
Lexington, KY   40506

University of Louisville,
Louisville, KY   40292

University of Lowell,
Lowell, MA   01854

University of Maine,
Orono, ME   04469

University of Mary
Hardin-Baylor,
Belton, TX   76513

University of Maryland,
Baltimore, MD   21228

University of Maryland,
College Park, MD   20742

University of Massachusetts,
Amherst, MA   01003

University of Miami,
Coral Gables, FL   33124

University of Michigan,
Ann Arbor, MI   48109

University of Michigan,
Dearborn, MI   48128

University of Minnesota,
Minneapolis, MN   55455

University of Mississippi,
University, MS   38677

University of Missouri,
Columbia, MO   65211

University of Missouri,
Kansas City, MO   64110

University of Missouri,
Rolla, MO   65401

University of Missouri,
St. Louis, MO   63121

University of Nebraska,
Lincoln, NE   68588

University of Nebraska,
Omaha, NE   68182

University of New Hampshire,
Durham, NH   03824

University of New Mexico,
Albuquerque, NM   87131

University of New Orleans,
New Orleans, LA   70148

University of North Carolina,
Chapel Hill, NC   27599

University of North Carolina,
Charlotte, NC   28223

University of North Carolina,
Greensboro, NC   27412

University of Northern
Colorado,
Greeley, CO   80639

University of Notre Dame,
Notre Dame, IN   46556

University of Oklahoma,
Norman, OK   73019

University of Oregon,
Eugene, OR   97403

University of the Pacific,
Stockton, CA   95211

University of Pennsylvania,
Philadelphia, PA   19104

University of Pittsburgh,
Greensburg, PA   15601

University of Pittsburgh,
Pittsburgh, PA   15260

University of Portland,
Portland, OR   97203

University of Redlands,
Redlands, CA   92373

University of Rochester,
Rochester, NY   14627

University of San Diego,
San Diego, CA   92110

University of San Francisco,
San Francisco, CA   94117

University of Scranton,
Scranton, PA   18510

University of South Alabama,
Mobile, AL   36688

University of South Carolina,
Columbia, SC   29208

University of Southern
California,
Los Angeles, CA   90089

University of Southern Maine,
Portland, ME   04103

University of Southern
Mississippi,
Hattiesburg, MS   39406

University of South Florida,
Tampa, FL   33620

University of Southwestern
Louisiana,
Lafayette, LA   70504

University of Tampa,
Tampa, FL   33606

University of Tennessee,
Knoxville, TN   37996

University of Texas,
Arlington, TX   76019

University of Texas,
Austin, TX   78712

University of Texas,
El Paso, TX   79968

University of Texas,
San Antonio, TX   78285

University of Toledo,
Toledo, OH   43606

University of Utah,
Salt Lake City, UT   84112

University of Vermont,
Burlington, VT   05405

University of Virginia,
Charlottesville, VA   22906

University of Washington,
Seattle, WA   98195

University of Wisconsin,
Madison, WI   53706

University of Wyoming,
Laramie, WY   82071

Upsala College,
East Orange, NJ   07019

Utah State University,
Logan, UT   84322

Valdosta State College,
Valdosta, GA   31698

Vanderbilt University,
Nashville, TN   37240

Villanova University,
Villanova, PA   19085

Virginia Military Institute,
Lexington, VA   24450

Virginia Polytechnic Institute
and State University,
Blacksburg, VA   24061

Wagner College,
Staten Island, NY   10301

Warner Pacific College,
Portland, OR   97215

Washburn University,
Topeka, KS   66621

Washington College,
Chestertown, MD   21620

Washington State University,
Pullman, WA   99164

Washington University,
St. Louis MO   63130

Wayne State University,
Detroit, MI   48202

Weber State College,
Ogden, UT   84408

Wellesley College,
Wellesley, MA   02181

Wells College,
Aurora, NY   13026

Wentworth Institute of
Technology,
Boston, MA   02115

West Chester University,
West Chester, PA   19383

Western Connecticut State
University,
Danbury, CT   06810

Western Kentucky University,
Bowling Green, KY   42101

Western Maryland College,
Westminster, MD   21157

Western New England College,
Springfield, MA   01119

Western Oregon State College,
Monmouth, OR   97361

Westminster College,
Salt Lake City, UT   84105

West Virginia University,
Morgantown, WV   26506

Whittier College,
Whittier, CA   90608

Widener University,
Chester, PA   19013

Wilkes College,
Wilkes-Barre, PA   18766

William Patterson College,
Wayne, NJ   07470

William Woods College,
Fulton, MO   65251

Wingate College,
Wingate, NC   28174

Wittenberg University,
Springfield, OH   45501

Worcester Polytechnic Institute,
Worcester, MA   01609

Worcester State College,
Worcester, MA   01602

Wright State University,
Dayton, OH   45435

Xavier University,
Cincinnati, OH   45207

Xavier University,
New Orleans, LA   70125

Yale University,
New Haven, CT   06520

ARMY
Abilene Christian University,
Abilene, TX   79699

Alabama Agricultural and
Mechanical University,
Normal, AL   35762

Albany State College,
Albany, GA   31705

Albright College,
Reading, PA   19612

Alcorn State University,
Lorman, MS   39096

Alderson-Broaddus College,
Philippi, WV   26416

Alfred University,
Alfred, NY   14802

Allegheny College,
Meadville, PA   16335

Allentown College of St.
Francis de Sales,
Center Valley, PA   18034

Alma College,
Alma MI   48801

Alverno College,
Reading, PA   19607

American International
College,
Springfield, MA   01109

American University,
Washington, DC   20016

Amherst College,
Amherst, MA   01002

Anna Maria College for
Men and Women,
Paxton, MA   01612

Appalachian State University,
Boone, NC   28608

Arizona State University,
Tempe, AZ   85287

Arkansas State University,
State University, AR   72467

Arkansas Tech University,
Russellville, AR   72801

Armstrong State College,
Savannah, GA   31419

Assumption College,
Worcester, MA   01615

Auburn University,
Auburn University, AL   38849

Augusta College,
Augusta, GA   30910

Aurora University,
Aurora, IL   60506

Austin Peay State University,
Clarksville, TN   37044

Baker University,
Baldwin City, KS   66006

Baldwin-Wallace College,
Berea, OH   44017

Ball State University,
Muncie, IN   47306

Barry University,
Miami Shores, FL   33161

Bellarmine College,
Louisville, KY   40205

Bellevue College,
Bellevue, NE 68005

Belmont Abbey College,
Belmont, NC 28012

Belmont College,
Nashville, TN 37212

Bemidji State University,
Bemidji, MN 56601

Benedict College,
Columbia, SC 29204

Benedictine College,
Atchison, KS 66002

Bentley College,
Waltham, MA 02154

Bethel College,
St. Paul, MN 55112

Bethune-Cookman College,
Daytona Beach, FL 32115

Biola University,
La Mirada, CA 90639

Birmingham-Southern College,
Birmingham, AL 35254

Black Hills State College,
Spearfish, SD 57783

Bloomfield College,
Bloomfield, NJ 07003

Bloomsburg University of
Pennsylvania,
Bloomsburg, PA 17815

Boise State University,
Boise, ID 83725

Boston College,
Chestnut Hill, MA 02167

Boston University,
Boston, MA 02215

Bowie State University,
Bowie, MD 20715

Bowling Green State
University,
Bowling Green, OH 43403

Bradley University,
Peoria, IL 61625

Bridgewater State College,
Bridgewater, MA 02324

Brigham Young University,
Provo, UT 84602

Brown University,
Providence, RI 02912

Bryant College,
Smithfield, RI 02917

Bryn Mawr College,
Bryn Mawr, PA 19010

Bucknell University,
Lewisburg, PA 17837

Butler University,
Indianapolis, IN 46208

Cabrini College,
Radnor, PA 19087

Caldwell College,
Caldwell, NJ 07006

California Institute of
Technology,
Pasadena, CA 91125

California Lutheran University,
Thousand Oaks, CA 91360

California Polytechnic State
University,
San Luis Obispo, CA 93407

California State Polytechnic
University,
Pomona, CA 91768

California State University,
Chico, CA 95929

California State University,
Fresno, CA 93740

California State University,
Fullerton, CA 92634

California State University,
Hayward, CA 94542

California State University,
Long Beach, CA 90840

California State University,
Northridge, CA 91330

California State University,
Sacramento, CA 95819

California University of
Pennsylvania,
California, PA 15419

Cameron University,
Lawton, OK 73505

Campbell University,
Bules Creek, NC 27506

Canisius College,
Buffalo, NY 14208

Capital University,
Columbus, OH 43209

Cardinal Stritch College,
Milwaukee, WI 53217

Carlow College,
Pittsburgh, PA 15213

Carnegie Mellon University,
Pittsburgh, PA 15213

Carson-Newman College,
Jefferson City, TN 37760

Carthage College,
Kenosha, WI 53140

Castleton State College,
Castleton, VT 05735

Catawba College,
Salisbury, NC 28144

Catholic University of America,
Washington, DC 20064

Cedar Crest College,
Allentown, PA 18104

Cedarville College,
Cedarville, OH 45314

Centenary College of
Louisiana,
Shreveport, LA 71134

Central Connecticut State
University,
New Britain, CT 06050

Central Methodist College,
Fayette, MO 65248

Central Michigan University,
Mt. Pleasant, MI 48859

Central Missouri State
University,
Warrensburg, MO 64093

Central State University,
Edmond, OK 73034

Central State University,
Wilberforce, OH 45384

Central Washington University,
Ellensburg, WA 98926

Chaminade University of
Honolulu,
Honolulu, HI 96816

Chatham College,
Pittsburgh, PA 15232

Chestnut Hill College,
Philadelphia, PA 19118

Chicago State University,
Chicago, IL 60628

Christian Brothers College,
Memphis, TN 38104

Christopher Newport College,
Newport News, VA 23606

The Citadel,
Charleston, SC 29409

City College of the University
of New York,
New York, NY 10031

Claflin College,
Orangeburg, SC 29115

Claremont McKenna College,
Claremont, CA 91711

Clarion University of
Pennsylvania,
Clarion, PA 16214

Clark College,
Atlanta, GA 30314

Clarke College,
Dubuque, IA 52001

Clarkson University,
Potsdam, NY 13676

Clark University,
Worcester, MA 01610

Clayton State College,
Morrow, GA 30260

Clemson University,
Clemson, SC 29634

Cleveland State University,
Cleveland, OH 44115

Coe College,
Cedar Rapids, IA 52402

Cogswell Polytechnical College,
Cupertino, CA 95014

Colby College,
Waterville, ME 04901

Colby-Sawyer College,
New London, NH 03257

College Misericordia,
Dallas, PA 18612

College of Idaho,
Caldwell, ID   83605

College of Mount St. Joseph,
Cincinnati, OH   45051

College of St. Benedict,
St. Joseph, MN   56374

College of St. Mary,
Omaha, NE   68124

College of St. Rose,
Albany, NY   12203

College of the Holy Cross,
Worcester, MA   01610

College of William and Mary,
Williamsburg, VA   23185

Colorado College,
Colorado Springs, CO   80903

Colorado School of Mines,
Golden, CO   80401

Colorado State University,
Fort Collins, CO   80523

Colorado Technical College,
Colorado Springs, CO   80907

Columbia College,
Columbia, SC   29203

Columbia University,
New York, NY   10027

Columbus College,
Columbus, GA   31993

Concordia College,
Moorhead, MN   56560

Concordia College,
St. Paul, MN   55104

Concordia Teachers College,
Seward, NE   68434

Converse College,
Spartanburg, SC   29301

Cornell University,
Ithaca, NY   14853

Creighton University,
Omaha, NE   68178

Cumberland College,
Williamsburg, KY   40769

Curry College,
Milton, MA   02186

Daemen College,
Amherst, NY   14226

Dakota State University,
Madison, SD   57042

Dallas Baptist University,
Dallas, TX   75211

Dartmouth College,
Hanover, NH   03755

David Lipscomb University,
Nashville, TN   37204

Davidson College,
Davidson, NC   28036

Delaware State College,
Dover, DE   19910

Delta State University,
Cleveland, MS   38733

DePauw University,
Greencastle, IN   46135

Dickinson College,
Carlisle, PA   17013

Dominican College of Blauvelt,
Orangeburg, NY   10962

Drake University,
Des Moines, IA   50311

Drew University,
Madison, NJ   07940

Drexel University,
Philadelphia, PA   19104

Drury College,
Springfield, MO   65802

Duke University,
Durham, NC   27706

Duquesne University,
Pittsburgh, PA   15282

D'Youville College,
Buffalo, NY   14201

East Carolina University,
Greenville, NC   27858

East Central University,
Ada, OK   74820

Eastern College,
Saint Davids, PA   19087

Eastern Connecticut State
University,
Williamantic, CT   06226

Eastern Illinois University,
Charleston, IL   61920

Eastern Kentucky University,
Richmond, KY   40475–3101

Eastern Michigan University,
Ypsilanti, MI   48197

Eastern Montana College,
Billings, MT   59101

Eastern New Mexico
University,
Portales, NM   88130

Eastern Oregon State College,
La Grande, OR   97850

Eastern Washington University,
Cheney, WA   99004

East Stroudsburg University of
Pennsylvania,
East Stroudsburg, PA   18301

East Tennessee State
University,
Johnson City, TN   37614

Eckerd College,
St. Petersburg, FL   33733

Edgewood College,
Madison, WI   53711

Edinboro University of
Pennsylvania,
Edinboro, PA   16444

Elizabeth City State University,
Elizabeth City, NC   27909

Elmhurst College,
Elmhurst, IL   60126

Elmira College,
Elmira, NY   14901

Elms College,
Chicopee, MA   01013

Elon College,
Elon College, NC   27244

Embry-Riddle Aeronautical
University,
Daytona Beach, FL   32114

Embry-Riddle Aeronautical
University,
Prescott, AZ   86301

Emmanuel College,
Boston, MA   02115

Emporia State University,
Emporia, KS   66801

Evangel College,
Springfield, MO   65802

Fairleigh Dickinson University,
Madison, NJ   86301

Fairleigh Dickinson University,
Rutherford, NJ   07070

Fairleigh Dickinson University,
Teaneck, NJ   07666

Fairmont State College,
Fairmont, WV   26554

Ferris State University,
Big Rapids, MI   49307

Fisk University,
Nashville, TN   37208

Fitchburg State College,
Fitchburg, MA   01420

Florida Agricultural and
Mechanical University,
Tallahassee, FL   32307

Florida Atlantic University,
Boca Raton, FL   33431

Florida Institute of Technology,
Melbourne, FL   32901

Florida International
University,
Miami, FL   33199

Florida Southern College,
Lakeland, FL   33801

Florida State University,
Tallahassee, FL   32306

Fontbonne College,
St. Louis, MO   63105

Fordham University,
Bronx, NY   10458

Fort Hays State University,
Hays, KS   67601

Fort Valley State College,
Fort Valley, GA   31030

Francis Marion College,
Florence, SC   29501

Franklin College of Indiana,
Franklin, IN   46131

Franklin University,
Columbus, OH   43215

Frostburg State University,
Frostburg, MD   21532

Furman University,
Greenville, SC   29613

Gannon University,
Erie, PA   16541

George Mason University,
Fairfax, VA   22030

Georgetown College,
Georgetown, KY   40324

Georgetown University,
Washington, DC   20057

Georgia Institute of
Technology,
Atlanta, GA   30332

Georgia Southern College,
Statesboro, GA   30460

Georgia Southwestern College,
Americus, GA   31709

Georgia State University,
Statesboro, GA   30458

Gettysburg College,
Gettysburg, PA   17325

Glassboro State College,
Glassboro, NJ   08028

Golden Gate University,
San Francisco, CA   94105

Goldey-Beacom College,
Wilmington, DE   19808

Gonzaga University,
Spokane, WA   99258

Gordon College,
Wenham, MA   01984

Goucher College,
Baltimore, MD   21204

Grand Canyon College,
Phoenix, AZ   85061

Grand Rapids Baptist College
and Seminary,
Grand Rapids, MI   49505

Grand View College,
Des Moines, IA   50316

Green Mountain College,
Poultney, VT   05764

Greensboro College,
Greensboro, NC   27401

Guilford College,
Greensboro, NC   27410

Gustavus Adolphus College,
St. Peter, MN   56082

Gwynedd-Mercy College,
Gwynedd Valley, PA   19437

Hamilton College,
Clinton, NY   13323

Hampden-Sydney College,
Hampden-Sydney, VA   23943

Hampton University,
Hampton, VA   23668

Hardin-Simmons University,
Abilene, TX   79698

Harvard University,
Cambridge, MA   02138

Harvey Mudd College,
Claremont, CA   91711

Hawaii Pacific College,
Honolulu, HI 96813

Henderson State University,
Arkadelphia, AR 71923

Hendrix College,
Conway, AR 72032

High Point College,
High Point, NC 27261

Hofstra University,
Hempstead, NY 11550

Hollins College,
Roanoke, VA 24020

Holy Names College,
Oakland, CA 94619

Hood College,
Frederick, MD 21701

Houghton College,
Houghton, NY 14744

Houston Baptist University,
Houston, TX 77074

Howard Payne University,
Brownwood, TX 76801

Howard University,
Washington, DC 20059

Huntingdon College,
Montgomery, AL 36194

Husson College,
Bangor, ME 04401

Idaho State University,
Pocatello, ID 83209

Illinois Benedictine College,
Lisle, IL 60532

Illinois Institute of Technology,
Chicago, IL 60616

Illinois State University,
Normal, IL 61761

Illinois Wesleyan University,
Bloomington, IL 61702

Incarnate Word College,
San Antonio, TX 78209

Indiana State University,
Terre Haute, IN 47809

Indiana University,
Bloomington, IN 47405

Indiana University Northwest,
Gary, IN 46408

Indiana University,
South Bend, IN 46634

Indiana University of
Pennsylvania,
Indiana, PA 15705

Indiana University Southeast,
New Albany, IN 47150

Indiana Wesleyan University,
Marion, IN 46953

Iona College,
New Rochelle, NY 10801

Iowa State University of
Science and Technology,
Ames, IA 50011

Jackson State University,
Jackson, MS   393217

Jacksonville State University,
Jacksonville, AL   36265

Jacksonville University,
Jacksonville, FL   32211

James Madison University,
Harrisburg, VA   22807

Jersey City State College,
Jersey City, NJ   07305

John Brown University,
Siloam Springs, AR   72761

John Carroll University,
University Heights,
OH   44118

Johns Hopkins University,
Baltimore, MD   21218

Johnson & Wales University,
Providence, RI   02903

Johnson C. Smith University,
Charlotte, NC   28216

Johnson State College,
Johnson, VT   05656

Kalamazoo College,
Kalamazoo, MI   49007

Kansas State University,
Manhattan, KS   66506

Kean College of New Jersey,
Union, NJ   07083

Kennesaw State College,
Marietta, GA   30061

Kent State University,
Kent, OH   44242

Kentucky State University,
Frankfort, KY   40601

King's College,
Wilkes-Barre, PA   18711

Knox College,
Galesburg, IL   61401

Knoxville College,
Knoxville, TN   37921

Kutztown University of
Pennsylvania,
Kutztown, PA   19530

Lafayette College,
Easton, PA   18042

Lamar University,
Beaumont, TX   77710

Lander College,
Greenwood, SC   29649

La Roche College,
Pittsburgh, PA   15237

La Salle University,
Philadelphia, PA   19141

Lawrence Technological
University,
Southfield, MI   48075

Lebanon Valley College,
Annville, PA   17003

Lehigh University,
Bethlehem, PA   18015

Le Moyne College,
Syracuse, NY   13214

Lewis-Clark State College,
Lewiston, ID   83501

Lewis University,
Romeoville, IL   60441

Liberty University,
Lynchburg, VA   24506

Lincoln Memorial University,
Harrogate, TN   37752

Lincoln University,
Jefferson City, MO   65101

Lincoln University,
Lincoln University, PA   19352

Lindenwood College,
St. Charles, MO   63301

Lindsey Wilson College,
Columbia, KY   42728

Lock Haven University of
Pennsylvania,
Lock Haven, PA   17745

Long Island University,
Brooklyn, NY   11201

Long Island University,
Southampton, NY   11968

Longwood College,
Farmville, VA   23901

Loras College,
Dubuque, IA   52001

Louisiana State University,
Shreveport, LA   71115

Louisiana State University and
Agricultural and Mechanical
College,
Baton Rouge, LA   70803

Loyola College,
Baltimore, MD   21210

Loyola Marymount University,
Los Angeles, CA   90045

Loyola University,
Chicago, IL   60611

Loyola University,
New Orleans, LA   70118

Lubbock Christian University,
Lubbock, TX   79407

Lycoming College,
Williamsport, PA   17701

Lynchburg College,
Lynchburg, VA   24501

Mankato State University,
Mankato, MN   56001

Manfield University of
Pennsylvania,
Mansfield, PA   16933

Marian College of
Fond du Lac,
Fond du Lac, WI   54935

Marietta College,
Marietta, OH   45750

Marist College,
Poughkeepsie, NY   12601

Marquette University,
Milwaukee, WI   53233

Marshall University,
Huntington, WV   25755

Maryland Institute
College of Art,
Baltimore, MD   21217

Marymount University,
Arlington, VA   22207

Maryville College,
St. Louis, MO   63141

Massachusetts College of
Pharmacy and Allied Health
Sciences,
Boston, MA   02115

Massachusetts Institute of
Technology,
Cambridge, MA   02139

Massachusetts Maritime
Academy,
Buzzards Bay, MA   02532

Mayville State University,
Mayville, ND   58257

McMurry College,
Abilene, TX   79697

McNeese State University,
Lake Charles, LA   70609

Medaille College,
Bufalo, NY   14214

Memphis State University,
Memphis, TN   38152

Mercer University,
Macon, GA   31207

Mercyhurst College,
Erie, PA   16546

Meredith College,
Raleigh, NC   27607

Mesa State College,
Grand Junction, CO   81502

Methodist College,
Fayetteville, NC   28311

Metropolitan State College,
Denver, CO   80204

Michigan State University,
East Lansing, MI   48824

Michigan Technological
University,
Houghton, MI   49931

Mid-America Nazarene
College,
Olathe, KS   66061

Middle Tennessee State
University,
Murfreesboro, TN   37132

Midland Lutheran College,
Fremont, NE   68025

Midwestern State University,
Wichita Falls, TX   76308

Millersville University of
Pennsylvania,
Millersville, PA   17551

Milligan College,
Milligan College, TN   37682

Millsaps College,
Jackson, MS   39210

Mills College,
Oakland, CA   94613

Milwaukee School of
Engineering,
Milwaukee, WI   53201

Mississippi College,
Clinton, MS   39058

Mississippi State University,
Mississippi State, MS   39762

Missouri Baptist College,
St. Louis, MO   63141

Missouri Southern State
College,
Joplin, MO   64801

Missouri Western State
College,
St. Joseph, MO   64507

Mobile College,
Mobile, AL   36613

Molloy College,
Rockville Centre, NY   11570

Monmouth College,
Monmouth, IL   61462

Monmouth College,
West Long Branch, NJ   07764

Montana State University,
Bozeman, MT   59717

Montclair State College,
Upper Montclair, NJ   07043

Moorhead State University,
Moorhead, MN   56560

Moravian College,
Bethlehem, PA   18018

Morehead State University,
Morehead, KY   40351

Morehouse College,
Atlanta, GA   30314

Morgan State University,
Baltimore, MD   21239

Morris Brown College,
Atlanta, GA   30314

Morris College,
Sumter, SC   29150

Mount Holyoke College,
South Hadley, MA   01075

Mount Mary College,
Milwaukee, WI   53222

Mount St. Mary's College,
Emmitsburg, MD   21727

Mount St. Mary's College,
Los Angeles, CA   90049

Mount Union College,
Alliance, OH   44601

Muhlenberg College,
Allentown, PA   18104

Murray State University,
Murray, KY   42071

Muskingum College,
New Concord, OH   43762

National University,
San Diego, CA   92108

Nazareth College,
Rochester, NY   14610

Nebraska Wesleyan University,
Lincoln, NE   68504

New England College,
Henniker, NH   03242

New Hampshire College,
Manchester, NH   33104

New Mexico Highlands
University,
Las Vegas, NM   87701

New Mexico Institute of
Mining and Technology,
Socorro, NM   87801

New Mexico State University,
Las Cruces, NM   88003

New York Institute of
Technology,
Old Westbury, NY   11568

New York University,
New York, NY   10011

Niagara University,
Niagara University,
NY   14109

Nicholls State University,
Thibodauz, LA   70310

Nichols College,
Dudley, MA   01570

Norfolk State University,
Norfolk, VA   23504

North Adams State College,
North Adams, MA   01247

North Carolina Agricultural
and Technical State University,
Greensboro, NC   27411

North Carolina Central
University,
Durham, NC   27707

North Carolina State
University,
Raleigh, NC   27695

North Carolina Wesleyan
College,
Rocky Mount, NC   27804

North Central College,
Naperville, IL   60566

North Dakota State University,
Fargo, ND   58105

Northeastern Illinois
University,
Chicago, IL   60625

Northeastern State University,
Tahlequah, OK   74464

Northeastern University,
Boston, MA   02115

Northeast Louisiana
University,
Monroe, LA   71209

Northeast Missouri State
University,
Kirksville, MO   63501

Northern Arizona University,
Flagstaff, AZ   86011

Northern Illinois University,
De Kalb, IL   60115

Northern Kentucky University,
Highland Heights, KY   41076

Northern Michigan University,
Marquette, MI   49855

North Georgia College,
Dahlonega, GA   30597

North Park College,
Chicago, IL   60625

Northrop University,
Los Angeles, CA   90045

Northwestern Oklahoma State
University,
Alva, OK   73717

Northwestern State University,
Natchitoches, LA   71497

Northwestern University,
Evanston, IL   60208

Northwest Missouri State
University,
Maryville, MO   64468

Northwest Nazarene College,
Nampa, ID   83686

Northwood Institute,
Midland, MI   48640

Norwich University,
Northfield, VT   05663

Notre Dame College,
Cleveland, OH   44121

Oakland University,
Rochester, MI   48309

Occidental College,
Los Angeles, CA   90041

Oglethorpe University,
Atlanta, GA   30319

Ohio Dominican College,
Columbus, OH   43219

Ohio State University,
Columbus, OH   43210

Ohio State University,
Lima, OH   45804

Ohio State University,
Mansfield, OH   44906

Ohio State University,
Marion, OH   43302

Ohio State University,
Newark, OH   43055

Ohio University,
Athens, OH   45701

Ohio University,
Chillicothe, OH   45601

Ohio University,
Lancaster, OH   43130

Oklahoma Christian College,
Oklahoma City, OK   73136

Oklahoma State University,
Stillwater, OK   74078

Old Dominion University,
Norfolk, VA   23529

Olivet Nazarene University,
Kankakee, IL   60901

Oral Roberts University,
Tulsa, OK   74171

Oregon Institute of
Technology,
Klamath Falls, OR   97601

Oregon State University,
Corvallis, OR   97331

Otterbein College,
Westerville, OH   43081

Ouachita Baptist University,
Arkadelphia, AR   71923

Our Lady of Holy Cross
College,
New Orleans, LA   70131

Pacific Lutheran University,
Tacoma, WA   98447

Pacific University,
Forest Grove, OR   97116

Pembroke State University,
Pembroke, NC   28372

Pennsylvania State University,
Erie, PA   16563

Pennsylvania State University,
University Park, PA   16802

Pepperdine University,
Malibu, CA   90265

Peru State College,
Peru, NE   68421

Pfeiffer College,
Misenheimer, NC   28109

Philadelphia College of
Pharmacy and Science,
Philadelphia, PA   19104

Pittsburg State University,
Pittsburg, KS   66762

Pitzer College,
Claremont, CA   91711

Plymouth State College,
Plymouth, NH   03264

Point Loma Nazarene College,
San Diego, CA   92106

Point Park College,
Pittsburgh, PA   15222

Polytechnic University,
Brooklyn, NY   11201

Polytechnic University,
Farmingdale, NY   11735

Pomona College,
Claremont, CA   91711

Portland State University,
Portland, OR   97207

Post College,
Waterbury, CT   06708

Prairie View A&M University,
Prairie View, TX   77446

Pratt Institute,
Brooklyn, NY   11205

Presbyterian College,
Clinton, SC   29325

Princeton University,
Princeton, NJ   08544

Providence College,
Providence, RI   02918

Purdue University,
West Lafayette, IN   47907

Queens College,
Charlotte, NC   28224

Radford University,
Radford, VA   24142

Ramapo College,
Mahwah, NJ   07430

Randolph-Macon College,
Ashland, VA   23005

Randolph-Macon Woman's
College,
Lynchburg, VA   24503

Reed College,
Portland, OR   97202

Regis College,
Denver, CO   80221

Rensselaer Polytechnic
Institute,
Troy, NY   12180

Rhode Island College,
Providence, RI   02908

Rice University,
Houston, TX   77251

Rider College,
Lawrenceville, NJ   08648

Ripon College,
Ripon, WI   54971

Roberts Wesleyan College,
Rochester, NY   14624

Rochester Institute of
Technology,
Rochester, NY   14623

Rockford College,
Rockford, IL   61108

Rockhurst College,
Kansas City, MO   64110

Roger Williams College,
Bristol, RI   02809

Rose-Hulman Institute of
Technology,
Terre Haute, IN   47803

Russell Sage College,
Troy, NY   12180

Rutgers,
New Brunswick, NJ   08903

Saginaw Valley State
University,
University Center, MI   48710

St. Anselm College,
Manchester, NH   03102

St. Augustine's College,
Raleigh, NC   27610

St. Bonaventure University,
St. Bonaventure, NY   14778

St. Cloud State University,
St. Cloud, MN   56301

St. Francis College,
Brooklyn Heights, NY   11201

St. Francis College,
Loretto, PA   15940

St. John Fisher College,
Rochester, NY   14618

St. John's University,
Collegeville, MN   56321

St. John's University,
Jamaica, NY   11439

St. Joseph College,
West Hartford, CT   06117

St. Joseph's College,
Brooklyn, NY   11205

St. Joseph's University,
Philadelphia, PA   19131

St. Lawrence University,
Canton, NY   13617

St. Leo College,
St. Leo, FL   33574

St. Louis College of Pharmacy,
St. Louis, MO   63110

St. Louis University,
St. Louis, MO   63103

St. Mary-of-the-Woods
College,
St. Mary-of-the-Woods,
IN   47876

St. Mary's College,
Moraga, CA   94575

St. Mary's College,
Notre Dame, IN   46556

St. Mary's College,
Winona, MN   55987

St. Mary's University,
San Antonio, TX   78228

St. Norbert College,
De Pere, WI   54115

St. Paul's College,
Lawrenceville, VA   23868

St. Peter's College,
Jersey City, NJ   07306

St. Thomas University,
Miami, FL   33054

St. Vincent College,
Latrobe, PA   15650

Salem College,
Winston-Salem, NC   27108

Salem State College,
Salem, MA   01970

Salisbury State University,
Salisbury, MD   21801

Salve Regina College,
Newport, RI   02840

Samford University,
Birmingham, AL   35229

Sam Houston State University,
Huntsville, TX   77341

San Diego State University,
San Diego, CA   92182

San Francisco State University,
San Francisco, CA   94132

San Jose State University,
San Jose, CA   95192

Santa Clara University,
Santa Clara, CA   95053

Savannah State College,
Savannah, GA   31404

Scripps College,
Claremont, CA   91711

Seattle Pacific University,
Seattle, WA   98119

Seattle University,
Seattle, WA   98122

Seton Hall University,
South Orange, NJ   07079

Seton Hill College,
Greensburg, PA   15601

Shawnee State University,
Portsmouth, OH   45662

Shepherd College,
Shepherdstown, WV   25443

Shippensburg University,
Shippensburg, PA   17257

Shorter College,
Rome, GA   30161

Siena College,
Loudonville, NY   12211

Simmons College,
Boston, MA   02115

Skidmore College,
Saratoga Springs, NY   12866

Slippery Rock University,
Slippery Rock, PA   16057

Smith College,
Northampton, MA   01063

South Dakota School of
Mines and Technology,
Rapid City, SD   57701

South Dakota State University,
Brookings, SD   57007

Southeastern College of the
Assemblies of God,
Lakeland, FL   33801

Southeastern Louisiana
University,
Hammond, LA   70402

Southeastern Massachusetts
University,
North Dartmouth,
MA   02747

Southeastern Oklahoma State
University,
Durant, OK   74701

Southeast Missouri State
University,
Cape Girardeau, MO   63701

Southern Arkansas University,
Magnolia, AR   71753

Southern College of
Technology,
Marietta, GA   30060

Southern Connecticut State
University,
New Haven, CT   06515

Southern Illinois University,
Carbondale, IL   62901

Southern Nazarene University,
Bethany, OK   73008

Southern Oregon State College,
Ashland, OR   97520

Southern Utah State College,
Cedar City, UT   84720

Southwest Baptist University,
Bolivar, MO   65613

Southwest Missouri State
University,
Springfield, MO   65804

Spalding University,
Louisville, KY   40203

Spelman College,
Atlanta, GA   30314

Springfield College,
Springfield, MA   01109

Spring Garden College,
Philadelphia, PA   19119

Spring Hill College,
Mobile, AL   36608

Stanford University,
Stanford, CA   94305

SUNY/College at Albany,
Albany, NY   12222

SUNY/College at Binghamton,
Binghamton, NY   13902

SUNY/College at Brockport,
Brockport, NY   14420

SUNY/College at Buffalo,
Buffalo, NY   14222

SUNY/College at Cortland,
Cortland, NY   13045

SUNY/College at Fredonia,
Fredonia, NY   14063

SUNY/College at Geneseo,
Geneseo, NY   14454

SUNY/College at New Paltz,
New Paltz, NY   12561

SUNY/College at
Old Westbury,
Old Westbury, NY   11568

SUNY/College at Oswego,
Oswego, NY   13126

SUNY/College at Potsdam,
Potsdam, NY   13676

Stephen F. Austin State
University,
Nacogdoches, TX   75962

Stephens College,
Columbia, MO   65215

Stetson University,
DeLand, FL   32720

Stevens Institute of
Technology,
Hoboken, NJ   07030

Stonehill College,
North Easton, MA   02357

Suffolk University,
Boston, MA   02108

Susquehanna University,
Selinsgrove, PA   17870

Sweet Briar College,
Sweet Briar, VA   24595

Syracuse University,
Syracuse, NY   13244

Tarleton State University,
Stephenville, TX   76402

Taylor University,
Upland, IN   46989

Temple University,
Philadelphia, PA   19122

Tennessee State University,
Nashville, TN   37209

Tennessee Technological
University,
Cookeville, TN   38505

Tennessee Temple University,
Chattanooga, TN   37404

Texas A&I University,
Kingsville, TX   78363

Texas A&M University,
College Station, TX   77843

Texas Christian University,
Fort Worth, TX   76129

Texas Lutheran College,
Seguin, TX   78155

Texas Southern University,
Houston, TX   77004

Texas Tech University,
Lubbock, TX   79409

Texas Wesleyan University,
Fort Worth, TX   76105

Texas Woman's University,
Denton, TX   76204

Thomas College,
Waterville, ME   04901

Thomas More College,
Crestview Hills, KY   41017

Tougaloo College,
Tougaloo, MS   39174

Towson State University,
Towson, MD   21204

Transylvania University,
Lexington, KY   40508

Trenton State College,
Trenton, NJ   08650

Trinity College,
Hartford, CT   06106

Trinity College,
Washington, DC   20017

Trinity University,
San Antonio, TX   78212

Tufts University,
Medford, MA   02155

Tulane University,
New Orleans, LA   70118

Tuskegee University,
Tuskegee, AL   36088

Union College,
Barbourville, KY   40906

Union College,
Schenectady, NY   12308

United States International
University,
San Diego, CA   92131

University of Akron,
Akron, OH   44325

University of Alabama,
Huntsville, AL   35899

University of Alabama,
Tuscaloosa, AL   35487

University of Alaska,
Fairbanks, AK   99775

University of Arizona,
Tucson, AZ   85721

University of Arkansas,
Little Rock, AR   72204

University of Arkansas,
Pine Bluff, AR   71601

University of Bridgeport,
Bridgeport, CT   06601

University of California,
Berkeley, CA   94720

University of California,
Davis, CA   95616

University of California,
Los Angeles, CA   90024

University of California,
Riverside, CA   92521

University of California,
San Diego, CA   92093

University of California,
Santa Barbara, CA   93106

University of Central Arkansas,
Conway, AR   72032

University of Central Florida,
Orlando, FL   32816

University of Charleston,
Charleston, WV   25304

University of Chicago,
Chicago, IL   60637

University of Cincinnati,
Cincinnati, OH   45221

University of Colorado,
Boulder, CO   90309

University of Colorado,
Colorado Springs, CO   80933

University of Colorado,
Denver, CO   80204

University of Connecticut,
Stamford, CT   06903

University of Connecticut,
Storrs, CT   06269

University of Dallas,
Irving, TX   75062

University of Dayton,
Dayton, OH   45469

University of Delaware,
Newark, DE   19716

University of Denver,
Denver, CO   80208

University of Detroit,
Detroit, MI   48221

University of the District of
Columbia,
Washington, DC   20008

University of Dubuque,
Dubuque, IA   52001

University of Florida,
Gainesville, FL   32611

University of Georgia,
Athens, GA   30602

University of Hartford,
West Hartford, CT   06117

University of Hawaii,
Hilo, HI   96720–4091

University of Hawaii,
Manoa, HI   96822

University of Houston,
Houston, TX   77004

University of Idaho,
Moscow, ID   83843

University of Illinois,
Chicago, IL   60680

University of Illinois at
Urbana-Champaign,
Urbana, IL   61801

University of Indianapolis,
Indianapolis, IN   46227

University of Iowa,
Iowa City, IA   52242

University of Kansas,
Lawrence, KS   66045

University of Kentucky,
Lexington, KY   40506

University of La Verne,
La Verne, CA   91750

University of Louisville,
Louisville, KY   40292

University of Lowell,
Lowell, MA   01854

University of Maine,
Orono, ME   04469

University of Maryland
Eastern Shore,
Princess Anne, MD   21853

University of Massachusetts,
Amherst, MA   01003

University of Massachusetts,
Boston, MA   02125

University of Miami,
Coral Gables, FL   33124

University of Michigan,
Ann Arbor, MI   48109

University of Michigan,
Dearborn, MI   48128

University of Minnesota,
Minneapolis, MN   55455

University of Mississippi,
University, MS   38677

University of Missouri,
Columbia, MO   65211

University of Missouri,
Kansas City, MO   64110

University of Missouri,
Rolla, MO   65401

University of Missouri,
St. Louis, MO   63121

University of Montana,
Missoula, MT   59812

University of Nebraska,
Lincoln, NE   68508

University of Nebraska,
Omaha, NE   68182

University of Nevada,
Las Vegas, NV   89154

University of Nevada,
Reno, NV   89557

University of New England,
Biddeford, ME   04005

University of New Hampshire,
Durham, NY   03824

University of New Haven,
West Haven, CT   06516

University of New Mexico,
Albuquerque, NM   87131

University of New Orleans,
New Orleans, LA   70148

University of North Alabama,
Florence, AL   35632

University of North Carolina,
Chapel Hill, NC   27599

University of North Carolina,
Charlotte, NC   28223

University of North Carolina,
Greensboro, NC   27412

University of North Carolina,
Wilmington, NC   28403

University of North Dakota,
Grand Forks, ND   58202

University of Northern
Colorado,
Greeley, CO   80639

University of Northern Iowa,
Cedar Falls, IA   50614

University of North Florida,
Jacksonville, FL   32216

University of Notre Dame,
Notre Dame, IN   46556

University of Oklahoma,
Norman, OK   73019

University of Oregon,
Eugene, OR   97403

University of the Ozarks,
Clarksville, AR   72830

University of Pennsylvania,
Philadelphia, PA   19104

University of Pittsburgh,
Bradford, PA   16701

University of Pittsburgh,
Greensburg, PA   15601

University of Pittsburgh,
Pittsburgh, PA   15260

University of Portland,
Portland, OR   97203

University of Puget Sound,
Tacoma, WA   98416

University of Redlands,
Redlands, CA   92373

University of Rhode Island,
Kingston, RI   02881

University of Richmond,
Richmond, VA   23173

University of Rochester,
Rochester, NY   14627

University of St. Thomas,
Houston, TX   77006

University of San Diego,
San Diego, CA   92110

University of San Francisco,
San Francisco, CA   94117

University of Scranton,
Scranton, PA   18510

University of South Alabama,
Mobile, AL   36688

University of South Carolina,
Aiken, SC   29801

University of South Carolina,
Columbia, SC   29208

University of South Carolina,
Spartanburg, SC   29303

University of South Dakota,
Vermillion, SD   57069

University of Southern
California,
Los Angeles, CA   90089

University of Southern
Colorado,
Pueblo, CO   81001

University of Southern Maine,
Portland, ME   04163

University of Southern
Mississippi,
Hattiesburg, MS   39406

University of South Florida,
Tampa, FL   33620

University of Tampa,
Tampa, FL   33606

University of Tennessee,
Chattanooga, TN   37403

University of Tennessee,
Knoxville, TN   37996

University of Tennessee,
Martin, TN   38238

University of Texas,
Arlington, TX   76019

University of Texas,
Austin, TX   78712

University of Texas,
El Paso, TX   79968

University of Texas,
San Antonio, TX   78285

University of Toledo,
Toledo, OH   43606

University of Tulsa,
Tulsa, OK   74104

University of Utah,
Salt Lake City, UT   84112

University of Vermont,
Burlington, VT   05405

University of Virginia,
Charlottesville, VA   22906

University of Washington,
Seattle, WA   98195

University of West Florida,
Pensacola, FL   32514

University of Wisconsin,
Green Bay, WI   54311

University of Wisconsin,
La Crosse, WI   54601

University of Wisconsin,
Madison, WI   53706

University of Wisconsin,
Milwaukee, WI   53201

University of Wisconsin,
Oshkosh, WI   54901

University of Wisconsin-
Parkside
Kenosha, WI   53141

University of Wisconsin,
Platteville, WI   53818

University of Wisconsin,
Stevens Point, WI   54481

University of Wisconsin
Whitewater, WI   53190

University of Wyoming,
Laramie, WY   82071

Upsala College,
East Orange, NJ   07019

Ursuline College,
Pepper Pike, OH   44124

Utah State University,
Logan, UT   84522

Valparaiso University,
Valparaiso, IN   46383

Vanderbilt University,
Nashville, TN   37240

Villanova University,
Villanova, PA   19085

Virginia Commonwealth
University,
Richmond, VA   23298

Virginia Military Institute,
Lexington, VA   24450

Virginia Polytechnic Institute
and State University,
Blacksburg, VA   24061

Virginia State University,
Petersburg, VA   23803

Virginia Union University,
Richmond, VA   23220

Viterbo College,
La Crosse, WI   54601

Wagner College,
Staten Island, NY   10301

Wake Forest University,
Winston-Salem, NC   27109

Washburn University of
Topeka,
Topeka, KS   66621

Washington and Jefferson
College,
Washington, PA   15301

Washington and Lee
University,
Lexington, VA   24450

Washington College,
Chestertown, MD   21620

Washington State University,
Pullman, WA   99164

Washington University,
St. Louis, MO   63130

Waynesburg College,
Waynesburg, PA   15370

Wayne State University,
Detroit, MI   48202

Weber State College,
Ogden, UT   84408

Wellesley College,
Wellesley, MA   02181

Wells College,
Aurora, NY   13026

Wentworth Institute of
Technology,
Boston, MA   02115

West Chester University,
West Chester, PA   19383

Western Carolina University,
Cullowhee, NC   28723

Western Connecticut State
University,
Danbury, CT   06810

Western Illinois University,
Macomb, IL   61455

Western Kentucky University,
Bowling Green, KY   42101

Western Maryland College,
Westminster, MD   21157

Western Michigan University,
Kalamazoo, MI   49008

Western New England College,
Springfield, MA   01119

Western Oregon State College,
Monmouth, OR   97361

Westfield State College,
Westfield, MA   01086

West Georgia College,
Carrollton, GA   30118

Westminster College,
Salt Lake City, UT   84105

Westminster College,
Wilmington, PA   16172

Westmont College,
Santa Barbara, CA   93108

West Texas State University,
Canyon, TX   79016

West Virginia Institute of
Technology,
Montgomery, WV   25136

West Virginia State College,
Institute, WV   25112

West Virginia University,
Morgantown, WV   26506

Wheaton College,
Norton, MA   02766

Wheaton College,
Wheaton, IL   60187

Wheeling Jesuit College,
Wheeling, WV   26003

Whittier College,
Whittier, CA   90608

Whitworth College,
Spokane, WA   99251

Wichita State University,
Wichita, KS   67208

Widener University,
Chester, PA   19103

Wilkes College,
Wilkes-Barre, PA   18766

William Woods College,
Fulton, MO   65251

Wilson College,
Chambersburg, PA   17201

Wingate College,
Wingate, NC   28174

Winona State University,
Winona, MN   55987

Winston-Salem State
University,
Winston-Salem, NC   27110

Winthrop College,
Rock Hill, SC   29733

Wittenberg University,
Springfield, OH   45501

Wofford College,
Spartanburg, SC   29301

Worcester Polytechnic Institute,
Worcester, MA   01609

Worcester State College,
Worcester, MA   01602

Wright State University,
Dayton, OH   45435

Xavier University,
Cincinnati, OH   45207

Xavier University,
New Orleans, LA   70125

Yale University,
New Haven, CT   06520

York College,
York, PA   17403

Youngstown State University,
Youngstown, OH   44555

NAVY
Agnes Scott College,
Decatur, GA   30030

American University,
Washington, DC   20016

Anna Maria College for
Men and Women,
Paxton, MA   01612

Armstrong State College,
Savannah, GA   31419

Art Academy of Cincinnati,
Cincinnati, OH   45202

Augsburg College,
Minneapolis, MN   55454

Belmont College,
Nashville, TN   37212

Bethel College,
St. Paul, MN   55112

Bloomfield College,
Bloomfield, NJ   07003

Boston College,
Chestnut Hill, MA   02167

Boston University,
Boston, MA   02215

Bryn Mawr College,
Bryn Mawr, PA   19010

California Institute of
Technology,
Pasadena, CA   91125

California State University,
Hayward, CA   94542

California State University,
Northridge, CA   91330

California State University,
Sacramento, CA   95819

Capital University,
Columbus, OH   43209

Carnegie Mellon University,
Pittsburgh, PA   15213

Catholic University of America,
Washington, DC   20064

Chicago State University,
Chicago, IL   60628

Christian Brothers College,
Memphis, TN   38104

The Citadel,
Charleston, SC   29409

Claremont McKenna College,
Claremont, CA   91711

Clark College,
Atlanta, GA   30314

Clark University,
Worcester, MA   01610

College of St. Rose,
Albany, NY   12203

College of the Holy Cross,
Worcester, MA   01610

Columbia College,
Columbia, SC   29203

Columbia University,
New York, NY   10027

Concordia College,
St. Paul, MN   55104

Concordia Teachers College,
Seward, NE   68434

Cornell University,
Ithaca, NY   14853

David Lipscomb University,
Nashville, TN   37204

Drexel University,
Philadelphia, PA   19104

Duke University,
Durham, NC   27706

Duquesne University,
Pittsburgh, PA   15282

Eastern Michigan University,
Ypsilanti, MI   48197

Elmhurst College,
Elmhurst, IL   60126

Embry-Riddle Aeronautical
University,
Prescott, AZ   86301

Fisk University,
Nashville, TN   37208

Florida Agricultural and
Mechanical University,
Tallahassee, FL   32307

Florida State University,
Tallahassee, FL   32306

Fordham University,
Bronx, NY   10458

Georgetown University,
Washington, DC   20047

George Washington University,
Washington, DC   20052

Georgia Institute of
Technology,
Atlanta, GA   30332

Georgia State University,
Statesboro, GA   30458

Golden Gate University,
San Francisco, CA   94105

Green Mountain College,
Poultney, VT   05764

Hampton University,
Hampton, VA   23668

Harvard University,
Cambridge, MA   02138

Houston Baptist University,
Houston, TX   77074

Howard University,
Washington, DC   20059

Illinois Benedictine College,
Lisle, IL   60532

Illinois Institute of Technology,
Chicago, IL   60616

Indiana University,
South Bend, IN   46634

Iowa State University of
Science and Technology,
Ames, IA   50011

Jacksonville University,
Jacksonville, FL   32211

Johnson State College,
Johnson, VT   05656

La Salle University,
Philadelphia, PA   19141

Lewis University,
Romeoville, IL   60411

Lindenwood College,
St. Charles, MO   63301

Louisiana State University and
Agricultural and Mechanical
College,
Baton Route, LA   70803

Loyola Marymount University,
Los Angeles, CA   90045

Loyola University,
Chicago, IL   60611

Loyola University,
New Orleans, LA   70118

Macalester College,
St. Paul, MN   55105

Marquette University,
Milwaukee, WI   53233

Massachusetts Institute of
Technology,
Cambridge, MA   02139

Memphis State University,
Memphis, TN   38152

Miami University,
Oxford, OH   45056

Mid-America Nazarene
College,
Olathe, KS   66061

Mills College,
Oakland, CA   94613

Morehouse College,
Atlanta, GA   30314

Morris Brown College,
Atlanta, GA   30314

Nazareth College,
Rochester, NY   14610

Nebraska Wesleyan University,
Lincoln, NE   68504

Norfolk State University,
Norfolk, VA   23504

North Carolina Central
University,
Durham, NC   27707

North Carolina State
University,
Raleigh, NC   27695

Northeastern University,
Boston, MA   02115

North Park College,
Chicago, IL   60625

Northrop University,
Los Angeles, CA   90045

Northwestern University,
Evanston, IL   60208

Northwood Institute,
Midland, MI   48640

Norwich University,
Northfield, VT   05663

Occidental College,
Los Angeles, CA   90041

Oglethorpe University,
Atlanta, GA   30319

Ohio Dominican College,
Columbus, OH   43219

Ohio State University,
Columbus, OH   43210

Ohio State University,
Lima, OH   45804

Ohio State University,
Mansfield, OH   44906

Ohio State University,
Marion, OH   43302

Ohio State University,
Newark, OH   43055

Old Dominion University,
Norfolk, VA   23539

Oregon State University,
Corvallis, OR   97331

Otterbein College,
Westerville, OH   43081

Pennsylvania State University,
University Park, PA   16802

Pepperdine University,
Malibu, CA   90265

Point Loma Nazarene College,
San Diego, CA   92106

Prairie View A&M University,
Prairie View, TX   77446

Purdue University,
West Lafayette, IN   47907

Rensselaer Polytechnic
Institute,
Troy, NY   12181

Rice College,
Houston, TX   77251

Roberts Wesleyan College,
Rochester, NY   14624

Rochester Institute of
Technology,
Rochester, NY 14623

Russell Sage College,
Troy, NY   12180

St. John Fisher College,
Rochester, NY   14618

St. Joseph's University,
Philadelphia, PA   19131

St. Mary's College,
Notre Dame, IN   46556

San Diego State University,
San Diego, CA   92182

San Francisco State University,
San Francisco, CA   94132

San Jose State University,
San Jose, CA   95192

Santa Clara University,
Santa Clara, CA   95053

Savanna State College,
Savannah, GA   31404

Seattle Pacific University,
Seattle, WA   98119

Seattle University,
Seattle, WA   98122

Siena College,
Loudonville, NY   12211

Skidmore College,
Saratoga Springs, NY   12866

Southern College of
Technology,
Marietta, GA   30060

Spelman College,
Atlanta, GA   30314

Stanford University,
Stanford, CA   94305

SUNY/College at Albany,
Albany, NY   12222

SUNY/College at Binghamton,
Binghamton, NY   13902

SUNY/College at Brockport,
Brockport, NY   14420

SUNY/College at Cortland,
Cortland, NY   13045

SUNY/College at Geneseo,
Geneseo, NY   14454

SUNY/Maritime College,
Throgs Neck, NY   10465

Stephens College,
Columbia, MO   65215

Taylor University,
Upland, IN   46989

Temple University,
Philadelphia, PA   19122

Tennessee State University,
Nashville, TN   37209

Texas A&M University,
College Station, TX   77843

Texas Southern University,
Houston, TX   77004

Texas Tech University,
Lubbock, TX   79409

Tufts University,
Medford, MA   02155

Tulane University,
New Orleans, LA   70118

Union College,
Schenectady, NY   12308

University of Arizona,
Tucson, Az   85721

University of California,
Berkeley, CA   94720

University of California,
Irvine, CA   92717

University of California,
Los Angeles, CA   90024

University of California,
San Diego, CA   92093

University of Chicago,
Chicago, IL   60637

University of Colorado,
Boulder, CO   80309

University of Colorado,
Denver, CO   80204

University of Findlay,
Findlay, OH   45840

University of Florida,
Gainesville, FL   32611

University of Houston,
Houston, TX   77004

University of Idaho,
Moscow, ID   83843

University of Illinois,
Chicago, IL   60680

University of Illinois at
Urbana-Champaign,
Urbana, IL   61801

University of Kansas,
Lawrence, KS   66045

University of Maine,
Orono, ME   04469

University of Michigan,
Ann Arbor, MI   48109

University of Michigan,
Dearborn, MI   48128

University of Minnesota,
Minneapolis, MN   55455

University of Mississippi,
University, MS   38677

University of Missouri,
Columbia, MO   65211

University of Nebraska,
Omaha, NE   68182

University of New Mexico,
Albuquerque, NM   87131

University of New Orleans,
New Orleans, LA   70148

University of North Carolina,
Chapel Hill, NC   27599

University of North Florida,
Jacksonville, FL   32216

University of Notre Dame,
Notre Dame, IN   46556

University of Oklahoma,
Norman, OK   73019

University of Pennsylvania,
Philadelphia, PA   19104

University of Rochester,
Rochester, NY   14627

University of San Diego,
San Diego, CA   92110

University of San Francisco,
San Francisco, CA   94117

University of Southern
California,
Los Angeles, CA   90089

University of Tennessee,
Knoxville, TN   37996

University of Texas,
Austin, TX   78712

University of Utah,
Salt Lake City, UT   84112

University of Virginia,
Charlottesville, VA   22906

University of Washington,
Seattle, WA   98195

University of Wisconsin,
Madison, WI   53706

University of Wisconsin,
Milwaukee, WI   53201

Vanderbilt University,
Nashville, TN   37240

Villanova University,
Villanova, PA 19085

Virginia Military Institute,
Lexington, VA 24450

Virginia Polytechnic Institute
and State University,
Blacksburg, VA 24061

Washington College,
Chestertown, MD 21620

Washington State University,
Pullman, WA 99164

Weber State College,
Ogden, UT 84408

Wellesley College,
Wellesley, MA 02181

Westminster College,
Salt Lake City, UT 84105

Whittier College,
Whittier, CA 90608

Worcester Polytechnic Institute,
Worcester, MA 01609

Worcester State College,
Worcester, MA 01602

Xavier University,
New Orleans, LA 70125

SCHOOLS OFFERING TUITION PAYMENT PLANS

Even when you have to pay up, it's not always as bad as having to write a check for the full amount your college has in mind. Check the school's payment options.

Some schools let you charge tuition payments to a credit card. Others allow you to pay tuition in installments or defer it for a time.

Here's our checklist.

ALABAMA

Alabama State University,
Montgomery 36195

Bessemer State Technical
College,
Bessemer 35021

Birmingham-Southern College,
Birmingham 35254

Faulkner University,
Montgomery 36193

Huntingdon College,
Montgomery 39193

International Bible College,
Florence 35630

Jacksonville State University,
Jacksonville 36265

Livingston University,
Livingston 35470

Samford University,
Birmingham 35229

Troy State University,
Dothan 36303

Troy State University,
Montgomery   36104

Tuskegee University,
Tuskegee   36088

University of Alabama,
Birmingham   35294

University of Alabama,
Tuscaloosa   35487

University of Montevallo,
Montevallo   35115

ALASKA
Alaska Pacific University,
Anchorage   99508

University of Alaska,
Anchorage   99508

University of Alaska,
Fairbanks   99775

University of Alaska,
Juneau   99801

ARIZONA
Arizona State University,
Tempe   85287

Arizona Western College,
Yuma   85366

Cochise College,
Douglas   85607

DeVry Institute of Technology,
Phoenix   85021

Eastern Arizona College,
Thatcher   85552

Embry-Riddle Aeronautical
University,
Prescott   86301

Grand Canyon University,
Phoenix   85061

Northern Arizona University,
Flagstaff   86011

Phoenix College,
Phoenix   85013

University of Arizona,
Tucson   85721

University of Phoenix,
Phoenix   85040

Western International
University,
Phoenix   85021

Yavapai College,
Prescott   86301

ARKANSAS
Arkansas College,
Batesville   72563

Arkansas Tech University,
Russellville   72801

Harding University,
Searcy   72143

Henderson State University,
Arkadelphia   71923

Hendrix College,
Conway   72032

John Brown University,
Siloam Springs   72761

Ouachita Baptist University,
Arkadelphia   71923

Southern Arkansas University,
Magnolia   71753

Southern Baptist College,
Walnut Ridge   72476

University of Arkansas,
Fayetteville   72701

University of Arkansas,
Little Rock   72204

CALIFORNIA
Allan Hancock College,
Santa Maria   93454

Art Center College of Design,
Pasadena   91103

Azusa Pacific University,
Azusa   91702

Biola University,
La Mirada   90639

California College of Arts
and Crafts,
Oakland   94618

California Institute of
Technology,
Pasadena   91125

California Lutheran University,
Thousand Oaks   91360

California State Polytechnic
University,
Pomona   91768

California State University,
Bakersfield   93311

California State University,
Chico   95929

California State University,
Dominguez Hills   90747

California State University,
Fresno   93740

California State University,
Hayward   94542

California State University
Los Angeles   90032

California State University,
Sacramento   95819

California State University,
San Bernardino   92407

California State University,
Stanislaus   95380

Canada Community College,
Redwood City   94061

Chapman College,
Orange   92666

Christian Heritage College,
El Cajon   92019

Claremont McKenna College,
Claremont   91711

Coleman College,
La Mesa   92041

College of Notre Dame,
Belmont   94002

College of the Sequoias,
Vialia   93277

Columbia College,
Columbia   95310

Cosumnes River College,
Sacramento   95823

De Anza College,
Cupertino   95104

DeVry Institute of Technology,
City of Industry   91746

Evergreen Valley College,
San Jose   95135

Fashion Institute of Design and
Merchandising,
Los Angeles   90017

Feather River College,
Quincy   95971

Fresno Pacific College,
Fresno   93702

Golden Gate University,
San Francisco   94105

Harvey Mudd College,
Claremont   91711

Heald Business College,
San Francisco   94103

Holy Names College,
Oakland   94619

Long Beach City College,
Long Beach   90808

Los Medanos College,
Pittsburg   94565

Loyola Marymount University,
Los Angeles   90045

Master's College,
Newhall   91322

Mendocino College,
Ukiah   95482

Mills College,
Oakland   94613

Mira Costa College,
Oceanside   92056

Mission College,
Santa Clara   95054

Moorpark College,
Moorpark   93021

Mount St. Mary's College,
Los Angeles   90049

Mount San Jacinto College,
San Jacinto   92383

Napa Valley College,
Napa   94558

National University,
San Diego   92108

Northrop University,
Los Angeles   90045

Occidental College,
Los Angeles   90041

Otis Art Institute of
Parsons School of Design,
Los Angeles   90057

Oxnard College,
Oxnard   93033

Pacific Union College,
Angwin   94508

Pepperdine University,
Culver City   90230

Pitzer College,
Claremont   91711

Point Loma Nazarene College,
San Diego   92106

Pomona College,
Claremont   91711

Porterville College,
Porterville   93257

Sacramento City College,
Sacramento   95822

Saddleback College,
Mission Viejo   92692

St. Mary's College,
Moraga   94575

San Bernardino Valley College,
San Bernardino   92410

San Diego City College,
San Diego   92101

San Diego Mesa College,
San Diego   92111

San Diego Miramar College,
San Diego   92126

San Diego State University,
San Diego   92182

San Francisco State University,
San Francisco   94132

San Jose City College,
San Jose   95128

San Jose State University,
San Jose   95192

Santa Clara University,
Santa Clara   95053

Santa Monica College,
Santa Monica   90405

Scripps College,
Claremont   91711

Sierra College,
Rocklin   95677

Skyline College,
San Bruno   94066

Sonoma State University,
Rohnert Park   94928

Southern California College,
Costa Mesa   92626

Stanford University,
Stanford   94305

United States International
University,
San Diego   92131

University of California,
Berkeley   94720

University of California,
Los Angeles   90024

University of La Verne,
La Verne   91750

University of San Diego,
San Diego   92110

University of San Francisco,
San Francisco   94117

University of Southern
California,
Los Angeles   90089

University of the Pacific,
Stockton   95211

Western State University,
Fullerton   92631

Westmont College,
Santa Barbara   93108

West Valley College,
Saratoga   95070

Woodbury University,
Burbank   91510

COLORADO
Adams State College,
Alamosa   81102

Colorado Christian University,
Lakewood   80226

Colorado College,
Colorado Springs   80903

Colorado Institute of Art,
Denver   80203

Colorado State University,
Fort Collins   80523

Colorado Technical College,
Colorado Springs   80907

Fort Lewis College,
Durango   81301

Metropolitan State College,
Denver   80204

Regis College,
Denver   80221

University of Colorado,
Denver   80204

University of Denver,
Denver   80208

University of Northern
Colorado,
Greeley   80639

University of Southern
Colorado,
Pueblo   81001

Western State College,
Gunnison   81230

CONNECTICUT
Central Connecticut State
University,
New Britain   06050

Charter Oak College,
Farmington   06032

Eastern Connecticut State
University,
Willimantic   06226

Hartford College for Women,
Hartford   06105

Post College,
Waterbury   06706

Quinnipiac College,
Hamden   06518

Sacred Heart University,
Bridgeport   06432

St. Joseph College,
West Hartford   06117

Trinity College,
Hartford   06106

University of Bridgeport,
Bridgeport   06601

University of Hartford,
West Hartford   06117

University of New Haven,
New Haven   06516

Wesleyan University,
Middletown   06457

Yale University,
New Haven   06520

DELAWARE
Delaware State College,
Dover   19901

Goldey Beacom College,
Wilmington   19808

University of Delaware,
Newark   19716

Wesley College,
Dover   19901

Wilmington College,
New Castle   19720

DISTRICT OF COLUMBIA
American University,
Washington   20016

Catholic University of America,
Washington   20064

Gallaudet University,
Washington   20002

George Washington University,
Washington   20052

Mount Vernon College,
Washington   20007

Southeastern University,
Washington   20024

Stayer College,
Washington   20005

Trinity College,
Washington   20017

University of the District of
Columbia,
Washington   20008

FLORIDA
Art Institute of
Fort Lauderdale,
Fort Lauderdale   33316

Barry University,
Miami Shores   33161

Bethune-Cookman College,
Daytona Beach   32115

Embry-Riddle Aeronautical
University,
Daytona Beach   32014

Florida Agricultural and
Mechanical University,
Tallahassee   32307

Florida Atlantic University,
Boca Raton   33433

Florida Institute of Technology,
Melbourne   32901

Florida Southern College,
Lakeland   33801

Florida State University,
Tallahassee   32308

Jacksonville University,
Jacksonville   32211

Nova University,
Fort Lauderdale   33314

Orlando College,
Orlando   32810

Palm Beach Atlantic College,
West Palm Beach   33402

Rollins College,
Winter Park   32789

St. Thomas University,
Miami   33054

Southeastern College of the
Assemblies of God,
Lakeland   33801

Tampa College,
Tampa   33614

University of Central Florida,
Orlando   32816

University of Florida,
Gainesville   32611

University of Miami,
Miami   33124

University of North Florida,
Jacksonville   32216

University of West Florida,
Pensacola   32514

GEORGIA
Abraham Baldwin Agricultural
College,
Tifton   31794

Agnes Scott College,
Decatur   30030

Albany State College,
Albany   31705

Augusta College,
Augusta   30910

Brenau Professional College,
Gainesville   30501

Brunswick College,
Brunswick   31523

Columbus College,
Columbus   31993

Darton College,
Albany   30720

DeVry Institute of Technology,
Decatur   30030

Emory University,
Atlanta   30322

Georgia Institute of
Technology,
Atlanta   30332

Georgia Southwestern College
Americus   31709

Gordon College,
Barnesville   30204

Mercer University,
Atlanta   30341

Morris Brown College,
Atlanta   30314

Oglethorpe University,
Atlanta   30319

Shorter College,
Rome   30161

Southern College of
Technology,
Marietta   30060

Toccoa Falls College,
Toccoa Falls   30598

HAWAII
Hawaii Pacific University,
Honolulu   96813

University of Hawaii,
Honolulu   96822

IDAHO
College of Idaho,
Caldwell   83605

College of Southern Idaho,
Twin Falls   83303

Lewis-Clark State College,
Lewiston   83501

Ricks College,
Rexburg   83440

ILLINOIS
Augustana College,
Rock Island   61201

Aurora University,
Aurora   60506

Barat College,
Lake Forest   60045

Belleville Area College,
Belleville   62221

Black Hawk College,
Moline   61265

Bradley University,
Peoria   61625

Carl Sandburg College,
Galesburg   61401

Chicago State University,
Chicago   60628

College of DuPage,
Glen Ellyn   60137

College of Lake County,
Grayslake   60030

College of St. Francis,
Joliet   60435

Columbia College,
Chicago   60605

Concordia University,
River Forest   60305

DePaul University,
Chicago   60604

DeVry Institute of Technology,
Chicago   60618

DeVry Institute of Technology,
Lombard   60148

Eastern Illinois University,
Charleston   61920

Elmhurst College,
Elmhurst 60126

Governors State University,
University Park 60466

Greenville College,
Greenville 62246

Illinois Benedictine College,
Lisle 60532

Illinois College,
Jacksonville 62650

Illinois Institute of Technology,
Chicago 60616

Kaskaskia College,
Centralia 62801

Kishwaukee College,
Malta 60150

Knox College,
Galesburg 61401

Lake Forest College,
Lake Forest 60045

Lake Land College,
Mattoon 61938

Lewis University,
Romeoville 60441

Loyola University,
Chicago 60611

McHenry County College,
Crystal Lake 60012

Midstate College,
Peoria 61602

Millikin University,
Decatur 62522

Moody Bible Institute,
Chicago 60610

Morton College,
Cicero 60650

Mundelein College,
Chicago 60660

National College of Education,
Evanston 60201

North Central College,
Naperville 60566

North Park College,
Chicago 60625

Northwestern University,
Evanston 60208

Olivet Nazarene University,
Kankakee 60901

Parks College, St. Louis,
Cahokia 62206

Prairie State College,
Chicago Heights 60411

Quincy College,
Quincy 62301

Robert Morris College,
Chicago 60601

Rockford College,
Rockford 61108

Rock Valley College,
Rockford 61101

Roosevelt University,
Chicago   60605

Rosary College,
River Forest   60305

St. Augustine College,
Chicago   60640

St. Xavier College,
Chicago   60655

Sangamon State University,
Springfield   62794

School of the Art Institute of
Chicago,
Chicago   60603

Southeastern Illinois College,
Harrisburg   62946

Southern Illinois University,
Carbondale   62901

South Suburban College of
Cook County—South
Suburban College,
S. Holland   60473

Trinity College,
Deerfield   60015

Triton College,
River Grove   60171

University of Chicago,
Chicago   60637

University of Illinois,
Chicago   60680

Western Illinois University,
Macomb   61455

Wheaton College,
Wheaton   60187

William Rainey Harper
College,
Palatine   60067

INDIANA
Anderson University,
Anderson   46012

Ball State University,
Muncie   47306

Butler University,
Indianapolis   46208

Calumet College of St. Joseph,
Whiting   46394

Earlham College,
Richmond   47374

Franklin College of Indiana,
Franklin   46131

Goshen College,
Goshen   46526

Hanover College,
Hanover   47243

Huntington College,
Huntington   46750

Indiana Institute of
Technology,
Fort Wayne   46803

Indiana State University,
Terre Haute   47809

Indiana University,
Bloomington   97405

Indiana Wesleyan University,
Marion   46953

ITT Technical Institute,
Indianapolis   46268

Lockyear College,
Evansville   47706

Manchester College,
N. Manchester   46962

Marian College, Marian,
Indianapolis   46222

Purdue University,
West Lafayette   47907

Rose-Hulman Institute of
Technology,
Terra Haute   47803

St. Francis College,
Fort Wayne   46808

St. Mary-of-the-Woods
College,
St. Mary-of-the-
Woods   47876

Summit Christian College,
Fort Wayne   46807

Tri-State University,
Angola   46703

University of Evansville,
Evansville   47722

University of Indianapolis,
Indianapolis   46227

University of Southern Indiana,
Evansville   47712

Vincennes University,
Vincennes   47591

Wabash College,
Crawfordsville   47933

IOWA

American Institute of Business,
Des Moines   50321

Briar Cliff College,
Sioux City   51104

Buena Vista College,
Storm Lake   50588

Central College,
Pella   50219

Clarke College,
Dubuque   52001

Coe College,
Cedar Rapids   52402

Cornell College,
Mount Vernon   52314

Drake University,
Des Moines   50311

Graceland College,
Lamoni   50140

Grinnell College,
Grinnell   50112

Iowa State University of
Science and Technology,
Ames   50011

Luther College,
Decorah   52101

Maharishi International
University,
Fairfield   52556

Marycrest College,
Davenport   52804

Morningside College,
Sioux City   51106

Northwestern College,
Orange City   51041

St. Ambrose University,
Davenport   52803

Simpson College,
Indianola   50125

University of Dubuque,
Dubuque   52001

University of Iowa,
Iowa City   52242

University of Northern Iowa,
Cedar Falls   50614

Upper Iowa University,
Fayette   52142

Vennard College,
University Park   52595

Wartburg College,
Waverly   50677

Westmar College,
Le Mars   51031

KANSAS
Baker University,
Baldwin City   66006

Benedictine College,
Atchison   29204

Bethany College,
Lindsborg   26032

Emporia State University,
Emporia   66801

Fort Hays State University,
Hays   67601

Friends University,
Wichita   67213.

Hesston College,
Hesston   67062

Kansas Newman College,
Wichita   67213

Kansas State University,
Manhattan   66506

Kansas Wesleyan,
Salina   67401

Mid-America Nazarene
College,
Olathe   66061

Ottawa University,
Ottawa   66067

Pittsburg State University,
Pittsburg   66762

St. Mary College,
Leavenworth   66048

University of Kansas,
Lawrence   66045

Washburn University,
Topeka   66621

Wichita State University,
Wichita   67208

KENTUCKY
Asbury College,
Wilmore   40390

Bellarmine College,
Louisville   40205

Brescia College,
Owensboro   42301

Centre College,
Danville   40422

Cumberland College,
Williamsburg   40769

Georgetown College,
Georgetown   40324

Kentucky Christian College,
Grayson   41143

Kentucky State University,
Frankfort   40601

Kentucky Wesleyan College,
Owensboro   42302

Lindsey Wilson College,
Columbia   42728

Murray State University,
Murray   42071

Northern Kentucky University,
Highland Heights   41076

Pikeville College,
Pikeville   41501

Spalding University,
Louisville   40203

Transylvania University,
Lexington   40508

Union College,
Barbourville   40906

University of Louisville,
Louisville   40292

Western Kentucky University,
Bowling Green   42101

LOUISIANA
Centenary College of
Louisiana,
Shreveport   71134

Dillard University,
New Orleans   70122

Grambling State University,
Grambling   71245

Louisiana College,
Pineville   71359

Louisiana Technical University,
Ruston   71272

Loyola University,
New Orleans   70118

Northeast Louisiana
University,
Monroe   71209

Northwestern State University,
Natchitoches   71497

Our Lady of Holy Cross
College,
New Orleans   70131

Southeastern Louisiana
University,
Hammond   70402

Xavier University of Louisiana,
New Orleans   70125

MAINE
Bowdoin College,
Brunswick   04011

Colby College,
Waterville   04901

College of the Atlantic,
Bar Harbor   04653

Husson College,
Bangor   04401

Southern Maine Technical
College,
South Portland   04106

Thomas College,
Waterville   04901

Unity College,
Unity   04988

University of Maine,
Augusta   04330

University of New England,
Biddeford   04005

University of Southern Maine,
Portland   04103

MARYLAND
Bowie State University,
Bowie   20715

Chesapeake College,
Wye Mills   21679

Columbia Union College,
Takoma Park   20912

Coppin State College,
Baltimore   21216

Frostburg State University,
Frostburg   21532

Hagerstown Junior College,
Hagerstown   21740

Hood College,
Frederick   21701

Johns Hopkins University,
Baltimore   21218

Loyola College,
Baltimore   21210

Montgomery College,
Rockville   20850

Morgan State University,
Baltimore   21239

Mount St. Mary's College,
Emmitsburg   21727

St. John's College,
Annapolis   21401

St. Mary's College of
Maryland,
St. Mary's City   20686

Towson State University,
Baltimore   21204

University of Baltimore,
Baltimore   21201

Villa Julie College,
Stevenson   21153

Washington Bible College,
Lanham   20706

Washington College,
Chestertown   21620

Western Maryland College,
Westminster   21157

MASSACHUSETTS
American International
College,
Springfield   01109

Anna Maria College for Men
and Women,
Paxton   01612

Assumption College,
Worcester   01615

Atlantic Union College,
South Lancaster   01561

Bentley College,
Waltham   02154

Berklee College of Music,
Boston   02215

Boston College,
Chestnut Hill   02167

Boston University,
Boston   02215

Brandeis University,
Waltham   02254

Bridgewater State College,
Bridgewater   02324

Elms College,
Chicopee   01013

Emerson College,
Boston   02116

Emmanuel College,
Boston   02115

Fitchburg State College,
Fitchburg   01420

Framingham State College,
Framingham   01701

Gordon College,
Wenham   01984

Hampshire College,
Amherst   01002

Harvard University,
Cambridge   02138

Massachusetts Institute of
Technology,
Cambridge   02139

Merrimack College,
North Andover   01845

Mount Holyoke College,
South Hadley   01075

Mount Ida College,
Newton Centre   02159

Nichols College,
Dudley   01570

North Adams State College,
North Adams   01247

Northeastern University,
Boston   02115

Pine Manor College,
Chestnut Hill   02167

Radcliffe College,
Cambridge   02138

Regis College,
Weston   02193

Salem State College,
Salem   01970

School of the Museum of
Fine Arts,
Boston   02115

Smith College,
Northampton   01063

Southeastern Massachusetts
University,
North Dartmouth   02747

Springfield College,
Springfield   01109

Suffolk University,
Boston   02108

Tufts University,
Medford   02155

University of Lowell,
Lowell   01854

Wellesley College,
Wellesley   02181

Western New England College,
Springfield   01119

Wheaton College,
Norton   02766

Wheelock College,
Boston   02215

Williams College,
Williamstown   01267

Worcester Polytechnic Institute,
Worcester   01609

Worcester State College,
Worcester   01602

MICHIGAN
Adrian College,
Adrian   49221

Albion College,
Albion   49224

Alma College,
Alma   48801

Andrews University,
Berrien Springs   49104

Aquinas College,
Grand Rapids   49506

Baker Junior College,
Flint   48507

Calvin College,
Grand Rapids   49546

Cleary College,
Ypsilanti   48197

Delta College,
University Center   48710

Detroit College of Business,
Dearborn   48126

Eastern Michigan University,
Ypsilanti   48197

Grand Rapids Baptist College
and Seminary,
Grand Rapids   49505

Grand Valley State University,
Allendale   49401

Hillsdale College,
Hillsdale   49242

Hope College,
Holland   49423

Jordan College,
Cedar Springs   49319

Kalamazoo College,
Kalamazoo   49009

Lake Michigan College,
Benton Harbor   49022

Lake Superior State University,
Sault Sainte Marie   49783

Lawrence Technological
University,
Southfield   48075

Madonna College,
Livonia   48150

Marygrove College,
Detroit   48221

Mercy College of Detroit,
Detroit   48219

Michigan State University,
East Lansing   48824

Northwestern Michigan
College,
Traverse City   49684

Oakland University,
Rochester   48309

Olivet College,
Olivet   49076

Saginaw Valley State
University,
University Center   48710

Schoolcraft College,
Livonia   48152

Siena Heights College,
Adrian   49221

Southwestern Michigan
College,
Dowagiac   49047

Spring Arbor College,
Spring Arbor   49283

University of Detroit,
Detroit   48221

University of Michigan,
Ann Arbor   48109

University of Michigan,
Dearborn   48128

University of Michigan,
Flint   48502

Walsh College of Accountancy
and Business Administration,
Troy   48007

Wayne State University,
Detroit   48202

MINNESOTA
Augsburg College,
Minneapolis   55454

Bemidji State University,
Bemidji   56601

Bethel College,
St. Paul   55112

Carleton College,
Northfield   55057

College of St. Catherine,
St. Paul   55105

College of St. Scholastica,
Duluth   55811

Concordia College,
Moorhead   56560

Concordia College,
St. Paul   55104

Hamline University,
St. Paul   55104

North Central Bible College,
Minneapolis   55404

Northwestern College,
St. Paul   55113

St. John's University,
Collegeville   56321

St. Mary's College,
Winona   55987

St. Olaf College,
Northfield   55057

Southwest State University,
Marshall   56258

University of Minnesota,
Minneapolis   55455

MISSISSIPPI
Alcorn State University,
Lorman   39096

Delta State University,
Cleveland   38733

Millsaps College,
Jackson   39210

Mississippi College,
Clinton   39058

Mississippi Gulf Coast Junior
College,
Perkinston   39573

Mississippi State University,
Mississippi State   39762

Mississippi University for
Women,
Columbus   39701

Mississippi Valley University,
Itta Bena   38941

Tougaloo College,
Tougaloo   39174

University of Mississippi,
University   38677

University of Southern
Mississippi,
Hattiesburg   39406

William Carey College,
Hattiesburg   39401

MISSOURI
Avila College,
Kansas City   64145

Baptist Bible College,
Springfield   65803

Central Bible College,
Springfield   65803

Central Methodist College,
Fayette 65248

Central Missouri State
University,
Warrensburg 64093

Culver-Stockton College,
Canton 63435

DeVry Institute of Technology,
Kansas City 64131

Drury College,
Springfield 65802

East Central College,
Union 63084

Evangel College,
Springfield 65802

Fontbonne College,
St. Louis 63105

Hannibal-LaGrange College,
Hannibal 63401

Harris Stowe State College,
St. Louis 63103

Jefferson College,
Hillsboro 63050

Lincoln University,
Jefferson City 65101

Lindenwood College,
St. Charles 63301

Maryville College,
St. Louis 63141

Missouri Baptist College,
St. Louis 63141

Missouri Southern State
College,
Joplin 64801

Missouri Valley College,
Marshall 65340

Missouri Western State
College,
St. Joseph 64507

Northeast Missouri State
University,
Kirksville 63501

Northwest Missouri State
University,
Maryville 64468

Rockhurst College,
Kansas City 64110

St. Louis Christian College,
St. Louis 63135

St. Louis University,
St. Louis 63103

Southeast Missouri State,
Cape Girardeau 63701

Southwest Baptist University,
Bolivar 65613

Southwest Missouri State
University,
Springfield 65804

Stephens College,
Columbia 65215

Tarkio College,
Tarkio 64491

University of Missouri,
Kansas City   64110

University of Missouri,
Rolla   65401

University of Missouri,
St. Louis   63121

Washington University,
St. Louis   63130

Webster University,
St. Louis   63119

William Jewell College,
Liberty   64068

William Woods College,
Fulton   65251

MONTANA
Carroll College,
Helena   59625

Eastern Montana College,
Billings   59101

Montana State University,
Bozeman   59717

University of Montana,
Missoula   59812

NEBRASKA
Bellevue College,
Bellevue   68005

Chadron State College,
Chadron   69337

College of St. Mary,
Omaha   68124

Concordia Teachers College,
Seward   68434

Creighton University,
Omaha   68178

Hastings College,
Hastings   68902

Midland Lutheran College,
Fremont   68025

Nebraska Wesleyan University,
Lincoln   68504

Peru State College,
Peru   68421

Union College,
Lincoln   68506

Wayne State College,
Wayne   68787

NEVADA
University of Nevada,
Las Vegas   89154

NEW HAMPSHIRE
Dartmouth College,
Hanover   03755

Franklin Pierce College,
Rindge   03461

Hesser College,
Manchester   03101

Keene State College,
Keene   03431

New Hampshire College,
Manchester   03104

New Hampshire Technical
Institute,
Concord   03302

Notre Dame College,
Manchester   03104

Rivier College,
Nashua   03063

University of New Hampshire,
Durham   03824

NEW JERSEY
Berkeley School of Garret
Mount,
West Paterson   07424

Bloomfield College,
Bloomfield   07003

Burlington County College,
Pemberton   08068

Caldwell College,
Caldwell   07006

Camden County College,
Blackwood   08012

Centenary College,
Hackettstown   07840

Cumberland County College,
Vineland   08360

Drew University,
Madison   07940

Fairleigh Dickinson University,
Madison   07940

Glassboro State College,
Glassboro   08028

Gloucester County College,
Sewell   08080

Jersey City State College,
Jersey City   07305

Kean College of New Jersey,
Union   07083

Monmouth College,
West Long Branch   07764

Montclair State College,
Upper Montclair   07043

New Jersey Institute of
Technology,
Newark   07102

Northeastern Bible College,
Essex Fells   07021

Princeton University,
Princeton   08544

Ramapo College of
New Jersey,
Mahwah   07430

Rider College,
Lawrenceville   08648

Rutgers/Cook College,
New Brunswick   08903

St. Peter's College,
Jersey City   07308

Seton Hall University,
South Orange   07079

Stockton State College,
Pomona   08240

Thomas A. Edison State
College,
Trenton   08625

Union County College,
Cranford   07016

Upsala College,
East Orange   07019

William Paterson College,
Wayne   07470

NEW MEXICO
College of Santa Fe,
Santa Fe   87501

Eastern New Mexico
University,
Portales   88130

New Mexico Highlands
University,
Las Vegas   87701

New Mexico Institute of
Mining and Technology,
Socorro   87801

New Mexico State University,
Las Cruces   88003

San Juan College,
Farmington   87401

University of New Mexico,
Albuquerque   87131

NEW YORK
Adelphi University,
Garden City   11530

Alfred University,
Alfred   14802

Bard College,
Annendale-on-Hudson   12504

Barnard College,
New York   10027

Canisius College,
Buffalo   14208

Cazenovia College,
Cazenovia   13035

City University of New York,
New York   10031

Clarkson College,
Potsdam   13676

College of Insurance,
New York   10007

College of New Rochelle,
New Rochelle   10805

College of St. Rose,
Albany   12203

Columbia University,
New York   10027

Cornell University,
Ithaca   14853

Daemen College,
Amherst   14226

Dominican College of Blauvelt,
Orangeburg   10962

Dowling College,
Oakdale   11769

D'Youville College,
Buffalo   14201

Elmira College,
Elmira   14901

Fashion Institute of
Technology,
New York   10001

Fordham University,
Bronx   10458

Hamilton College,
Clinton   13323

Hobart College,
Geneva   14456

Houghton College,
Houghton   14744

Iona College,
New Rochelle   10801

Le Moyne College,
Syracuse   13214

Long Island University,
Brooklyn   11201

Manhattan College,
Riverdale   10471

Manhattan School of Music,
New York   10027

Manhattanville College,
Purchase   10577

Mannes College of Music,
New York   10024

Marymount Manhattan
College,
New York   10021

Medaille College,
Buffalo   14214

Mercy College,
Dobbs Ferry   10522

Molloy College,
Rockville Centre   11570

Nazareth College of Rochester,
Rochester   14610

New York Institute of
Technology,
Old Westbury   11568

New York University,
New York   10003

Niagara University,
Niagara University   14109

Nyack College,
Nyack   10960

Pace University,
New York   10038

Parsons School of Design,
New York   10011

Polytechnic University,
Brooklyn   11201

Pratt Institute,
Brooklyn   11205

Rensselaer Polytechnic
Institute,
Troy   12180

Rochester Institute of
Technology,
Rochester   14623

Russell Sage College,
Troy   12180

St. John Fisher,
Rochester   14618

St. Francis College,
Brooklyn Heights   11201

St. Joseph's College,
Brooklyn   11205

St. Thomas Aquinas College,
Sparkill   10976

Sarah Lawrence College,
Bronxville   10708

School of Visual Arts,
New York   10010

Siena College,
Loudonville   12211

Skidmore College,
Saratoga Springs   12866

SUNY/College at Brockport,
Brockport   14420

SUNY/College at Buffalo,
Buffalo   14260

SUNY/College at Cortland,
Cortland   13045

SUNY/College at Fredonia,
Fredonia   14063

SUNY/College at Geneseo,
Geneseo   14454

SUNY/College at New Paltz,
New Paltz   12561–2499

SUNY/College at Old
Westbury,
Old Westbury   11568–0210

SUNY/College at Oswego,
Oswego   13126

SUNY/College at Plattsburgh,
Plattsburgh   12901

SUNY/College at Potsdam,
Potsdam   13676

SUNY/College of Technology
at Alfred,
Alfred   14802

SUNY/College of Technology
at Canton,
Canton   13617

SUNY/College of Technology
at Farmingdale,
Farmingdale   11735

Syracuse University,
Syracuse   13244

Touro College,
New York   10001

University of Rochester,
Rochester   14627

Utica College,
Utica   13502

Vassar College,
Poughkeepsie   12601

Wagner College,
Staten Island   10301

Wells College,
Aurora   13026

William Smith College,
Geneva 14456

NORTH CAROLINA
Appalachian State University,
Boone 28608

Atlantic Christian College,
Wilson 27893

Belmont Abbey College,
Belmont 28012

Campbell University,
Buies Creek 27506

Catawba College,
Salisbury 28144

Chowan College,
Murfreesboro 27855

Davidson College,
Davidson 28036

Duke University,
Durham 27706

Elon College,
Elon College 27244

Fayetteville State University,
Fayetteville 28301

Gardner-Webb College,
Boiling Springs 28017

Gaston College,
Dallas 28034

Guilford College,
Greensboro 27410

Lees-McRae College,
Banner Elk 28604

Lenoir-Rhyne College,
Hickory 28603

Louisburg College,
Louisburg 27549

Mars Hill College,
Mars Hill 28754

Meredith College,
Raleigh 27607

Methodist College,
Fayetteville 28311

Mount Olive College,
Mount Olive 28365

North Carolina State
University,
Greensboro 27411

North Carolina Central
University,
Durham 27707

North Carolina Wesleyan
College,
Rocky Mount 27804

Pfeiffer College,
Misenheimer 28109

Queens College,
Charlotte 28274

St. Andrews Presbyterian
College,
Laurinburg 28352

St. Augustine's College,
Raleigh 27610

Salem College,
Winston-Salem 27108

University of North Carolina,
Chapel Hill   27599

Wake Forest University,
Winston-Salem   27109

Wingate College,
Wingate   28174

Winston-Salem State
University,
Winston-Salem   27110

NORTH DAKOTA
Jamestown College,
Jamestown   58401

Mayville State University,
Mayville   58257

University of Mary,
Bismarck   58504

University of North Dakota,
Grand Forks   58202

OHIO
Ashland College,
Ashland   44805

Baldwin-Wallace College,
Berea   44017

Bowling Green State
University,
Bowling Green   43403

Capital University,
Columbus   43209

Case Western Reserve
University,
Cleveland   44106

Cedarville College,
Cedarville   45314

Central Ohio Technical
College,
Newark   43055

Central State University,
Wilberforce   45384

Cincinnati Bible College and
Seminary,
Cincinnati   45204

Circleville Bible College,
Circleville   43113

Cleveland State University,
Cleveland   44115

College of Mount St. Joseph,
Cincinnati   45051

College of Wooster,
Wooster   44691

Columbus College of Art and
Design,
Columbus   43215

Defiance College,
Defiance   43512

Denison University,
Granville   43023

DeVry Institute of Technology,
Columbus   43209

Dyke College,
Cleveland   44118

Franciscan University of
Steubenville,
Steubenville   43952

Franklin University,
Columbus 43215

Heidelberg College,
Tiffin 44883

Hiram College,
Hiram 44234

Jefferson Technical College,
Steubenville 43952

John Carroll University,
Cleveland 44118

Kent State University,
Kent 44242

Kenyon College,
Gambier 43022

Lake Erie College,
Painesville 44077

Lourdes College,
Sylvania 43560

Malone College,
Canton 44709

Marietta College,
Marietta 45750

Marion Technical College,
Marion 43302

Miami University,
Oxford 45046

Mount Union College,
Alliance 44601

Mount Vernon Nazarene
College,
Mount Vernon 43050

Muskingum College,
New Concord 43762

North Central Technical
College,
Mansfield 44906

Northwestern Business College
and Technical Center,
Lima 45805

Northwest Technical College,
Archbold 43502

Notre Dame College,
Cleveland 44121

Oberlin College,
Oberlin 44074

Ohio Dominican College,
Columbus 43219

Ohio Northern University,
Ada 45810

Ohio State University,
Columbus 43210

Ohio University,
Athens 45701

Ohio Wesleyan University,
Delaware 43015

Otterbein College,
Westerville 43081

Shawnee State University,
Portsmouth 45662

Stark Technical College,
Canton 44720

Terra Technical College,
Fremont   43420

Tiffin University,
Tiffin   44883

Union Institute,
Cincinnati   45202

University of Akron,
Akron   44325

University of Cincinnati,
Cincinnati   45221

University of Dayton,
Dayton   45469

University of Findlay,
Findlay   45840

University of Rio Grande,
Rio Grande   45674

University of Toledo,
Toledo   43606

Urbana University,
Urbana   43078

Ursuline College,
Pepper Pike   44124

Walsh College,
Canton   44720

Washington Technical College,
Marietta   45750

Wilberforce University,
Wilberforce   45384

Wilmington College,
Wilmington   45177

Wittenberg University,
Springfield   45501

Wright State University,
Dayton   45435

Xavier University,
Cincinnati   45207

Youngstown State University,
Youngstown   44555

OKLAHOMA
Cameron University,
Lawton   73505

Connors State College,
Warren   74469

East Central University,
Ada   74820

Northern Oklahoma College,
Tonkawa   74653

Northwestern Oklahoma State
University,
Alva   73717

Oklahoma Christian College,
Oklahoma City   73136

Oklahoma City University,
Oklahoma City   73106

Oklahoma Panhandle State
University,
Goodwell   73939

Oklahoma State University,
Stillwater   74078

Phillips University,
Enid   73701

Rogers State College,
Claremore 74017

Southern Nazarene University,
Bethany 73008

Southeastern Oklahoma State
University,
Durant 74701

University of Oklahoma,
Norman 73019

University of Tulsa,
Tulsa 74104

OREGON
George Fox College,
Newberg 97132

Lewis and Clark College,
Portland 97219

Linfield College,
McMinnville 97128

Maryhurst College,
Maryhurst 97036

Oregon Institute of
Technology,
Klamath Falls 97601

Oregon State University,
Corvallis 97331

Pacific University,
Forest Grove 97116

Portland State University,
Portland 97207

Reed College,
Portland 97202

University of Oregon,
Eugene 97403

University of Portland,
Portland 97203

Western Oregon State College,
Monmouth 97361

Willamette University,
Salem 97301

PENNSYLVANIA
Academy of the New Church,
Bryn Athyn 19009

Albright College,
Reading 19612

Allegheny College,
Meadville 16335

Alvernia College,
Reading 19607

Art Institute of Pittsburgh,
Pittsburgh 15222

Beaver College,
Glenside 19038

Bryn Mawr College,
Bryn Mawr 19010

Bucknell University,
Lewisburg 17837

Cabrini College,
Radnor 19087

Carlow College,
Pittsburgh 15213

Carnegie Mellon University,
Pittsburgh 15213

Cedar Crest College,
Allentown   18104

Chestnut Hill College,
Philadelphia   19118

Cheyney University,
Cheyney   19319

College Misericordia,
Dallas   18612

Delaware Valley College of
Science and Agriculture,
Doylestown   18901

Dickinson College,
Carlisle   17013

Duquesne University,
Pittsburgh   15282

Eastern College,
Saint Davids   19087

Elizabethtown College,
Elizabethtown   17022

Franklin and Marshall College,
Lancaster   17604

Gannon University,
Erie   16541

Geneva College,
Beaver Falls   15010

Gettysburg College,
Gettysburg   17325

Gwynedd-Mercy College,
Gwynedd Valley   19437

Hahnemann University,
Philadelphia   19102

Haverford College,
Haverford   19041

Holy Family College,
Philadelphia   19114

ICS Center for Degree Studies,
Scranton   18515

Indiana University of
Pennsylvania,
Indiana   15705

King's College,
Wilkes-Barre   18711

Kutztown University of
Pennsylvania,
Kutztown   19530

La Roche College,
Pittsburgh   15237

La Salle University,
Philadelphia   19141

Lebanon Valley College,
Annville   17003

Marywood College,
Scranton   18509

Mercyhurst College,
Erie   16546

Messiah College,
Grantham   17027

Millersville University of
Pennsylvania,
Millersville   17551

Philadelphia College of
Pharmacy and Science,
Philadelphia   19104

Philadelphia College of Textiles
and Science,
Philadelphia 19144

Point Park College,
Pittsburgh 15222

Robert Morris College,
Coraopolis 15108

St. Francis College,
Loretto 15940

St. Joseph's University,
Philadelphia 19131

Seton Hill College,
Greensburg 15601

Spring Garden College,
Philadelphia 19119

Swarthmore College,
Swarthmore 19081

Temple University,
Philadelphia 19122

Thiel College,
Greenville 16125

Thomas Jefferson University,
Philadelphia 19107

University of Pennsylvania,
Philadelphia 19104

University of Pittsburgh,
Pittsburgh 15260

University of Scranton,
Scranton 18510

University of the Arts,
Philadelphia 19102

Ursinus College,
Collegeville 19426

Villanova University,
Villanova 19085

West Chester University of
Pennsylvania,
West Chester 19383

Widener College of Widener
University,
Chester 19013

Wilkes University,
Wilkes-Barre 18766

Wilson College,
Chambersburg 17201

RHODE ISLAND
Brown University,
Providence 02912

Bryant College,
Smithfield 02917

Johnson & Wales University,
Providence 02903

New England Institute of
Technology,
Warwick 02886

Providence College,
Providence 02918

Rhode Island College,
Providence 02908

Rhode Island School of Design,
Providence 02903

Roger Williams College,
Bristol 02809

Salve Regina College,
Newport   02840

SOUTH CAROLINA
Anderson College,
Anderson   29621

Baptist College,
Charleston   29411

Benedict College,
Columbia   29204

Bob Jones University,
Greenville   29614

The Citadel,
Charleston   29409

Claflin College,
Orangeburg   29115

Clemson University,
Clemson   29634

College of Charleston,
Charleston   29424

Columbia College,
Columbia   29203

Converse College,
Spartanburg   29301

Florence-Darlington Technical
College,
Florence   29501

Francis Marion College,
Florence   29501

Furman University,
Greenville   29613

Greenville Technical College,
Greenville   29606

Horry-Georgetown Technical
College,
Conway,   29526

Lander College,
Greenwood   29649

Limestone College,
Gaffney   29340

Morris College,
Sumter   29150

Piedmont Technical College,
Greenwood   29648

Presbyterian College,
Clinton   29325

Spartanburg Technical College,
Spartanburg   29305

Sumter Area Technical College,
Sumter   29150

University of South Carolina,
Columbia   29208

Winthrop College,
Rock Hill   29733

York Technical College,
Rock Hill   29730

SOUTH DAKOTA
Augustana College,
Sioux Falls   57197

Black Hills State College,
Spearfish   57783

Dakota State University,
Madison   57042

Northern State College,
Aberdeen   57401

Oglala Lakota College,
Kyle   57752

Sioux Falls College,
Sioux Falls   57105

South Dakota School of Mines
and Technology,
Rapid City   57701

South Dakota State University,
Brookings   57007

University of South Dakota,
Vermillion   57069

TENNESSEE
Belmont College,
Nashville   37212

Carson-Newman College,
Jefferson City   37760

David Lipscomb University,
Nashville   37204

East Tennessee State
University,
Johnson City   37614

Fisk University,
Nashville   37208

Freed-Hardeman College,
Henderson   38340

Knoxville College,
Knoxville   37921

Lambuth College,
Jackson   38301

Lee College,
Cleveland   37311

LeMoyne-Owen College,
Memphis   38126

Lincoln Memorial University,
Harrogate   37752

Maryville College,
Maryville   37801

Memphis State University,
Memphis   38152

Middle Tennessee State
University,
Murfreesboro   37132

Milligan College,
Milligan   37682

Nashville State Technical
Institute,
Nashville   37209

Rhodes College,
Memphis   38112

Southern College of Seventh-
Day Adventists,
Collegedale   37315

State Technical Institute at
Memphis,
Memphis   38134

Tennessee State University,
Nashville   37209

Tennessee Technological
University,
Cookeville   38505

Tennessee Temple University,
Chattanooga   37404

Trevecca Nazarene College,
Nashville   37210

Tri-Cities State Technical
Institute,
Blountville   37617

Tusculumn College,
Greeneville   37743

University of the South,
Sewanee   37375

University of Tennessee,
Chattanooga   37403

University of Tennessee,
Knoxville   37996

University of Tennessee,
Memphis   38163

TEXAS
Abilene Christian University,
Abilene   79699

Amarillo College,
Amarillo   79178

Angelina College,
Lufkin   75902

Angelo State University,
San Angelo   76909

Austin College,
Sherman   75091

Brookhaven College,
Farmers Branch   75244

Cedar Valley College,
Lancaster   75134

Dallas Baptist University,
Dallas   75211

Del Mar College,
Corpus Christi   78404

Eastfield College,
Mesquite   75150

East Texas Baptist University,
Marshall   75670

El Centro College,
Dallas   75202

Hardin-Simmons University,
Abilene   79698

Howard College,
Big Spring   79720

Howard Payne University,
Brownwood   76801

Huston-Tillotson College,
Austin   78702

Incarnate Word College,
San Antonio   78209

Lamar University,
Beaumont   77710

Laredo State University,
Laredo   78040

Lee College,
Cleveland   37311

Lon Morris College,
Jacksonville   75766

Lubbock Christian Academy,
Lubbock   79407

McMurry College,
Abilene   79697

Midwestern State University,
Witchita Falls   76308

Mountain View College,
Dallas   75211

Navarro College,
Corsicana   75110

Odessa College,
Odessa   79764

Our Lady of the Lake
University,
San Antonio   78207

Prairie View A&M University,
Prairie View   77446

Rice University,
Houston   77251

St. Edward's University,
Austin   78704

St. Mary's University,
San Antonio   78228

St. Philip's College,
San Antonio   78203

Sam Houston State University,
Huntsville   77341

San Jacinto College North,
Houston   77049

Schreiner College,
Kerrville   78028

Southern Methodist University,
Dallas   75275

Southwestern Adventist
College,
Keene   76059

Southwestern Assemblies of
God College,
Waxahachie   75165

Southwest Texas State
University,
San Marcos   78666

Stephen F. Austin
State University,
Nacogdoches   75962

Sul Ross State University,
Alpine   79832

Tarleton State University,
Stephenville   76402

Texas A&I University,
Kingsville   78363

Texas A&M University,
College Station   77843

Texas Christian University,
Fort Worth   76129

Texas Lutheran College,
Seguin   78155

Texas Southern University,
Houston   77004

Texas State Technical Institute,
Harlingen   78551

Texas Tech University,
Lubbock   79409

Texas Wesleyan College,
Fort Worth   76105

Texas Woman's University,
Denton   76204

University of Dallas,
Irving   75062

University of Houston,
Houston   77004

University of Mary Hardin-
Baylor,
Belton   76513

University of North Texas,
Denton   76203

University of Texas,
Arlington   76019

University of Texas,
Austin   78712

University of Texas,
Richardson   75083

University of Texas,
El Paso   79968

University of Texas,
Permian Basin,
Odessa   79762

University of Texas,
San Antonio   78285

University of Texas,
Tyler   75701

Wayland Baptist University,
Plain View   79072

Western Texas College,
Snyder   79549

UTAH
University of Utah,
Salt Lake City   84112

Utah State University,
Logan   84322

Westminster College,
Salt Lake City   84105

VERMONT
Bennington College,
Bennington   05201

Champlain College,
Burlington   05402

Johnson State College,
Johnson   05656

Lyndon State College,
Lyndonville   05851

Norwich University,
Northfield   05663

St. Michael's College,
Colchester   05439

Southern Vermont College,
Bennington   05201

Trinity College of Vermont,
Burlington   05401

University of Vermont,
Burlington   05405

VIRGINIA
Averett College,
Danville   24541

Christopher Newport College,
Newport News   23606

Clinch Valley College,
Wise   24293

College of William and Mary,
Williamsburg   23185

Emory and Henry College,
Emory   24327

Ferrum College,
Ferrum   24088

George Mason University,
Fairfax   22030

Hampden-Sydney College,
Hampden-Sydney   23943

Hampton University,
Hampton   23668

Hollins College,
Roanoke   24020

James Madison University,
Harrisonburg   22807

Liberty University,
Lynchburg   24506

Longwood College,
Farmville   23901

Lynchburg College,
Lynchburg   24501

Marymount University,
Arlington   22207

Norfolk State University,
Norfolk   23504

Old Dominion University,
Norfolk   23529

Radford University,
Radford   24142

Randolph-Macon College,
Ashland   23005

Randolph-Macon Woman's
College,
Lynchburg   24503

Richard Bland College,
Petersburg   23805

Roanoke College,
Salem   24153

Shenandoah College and
Conservatory,
Winchester   22601

Sweet Briar College,
Sweet Briar   24595

Virginia Commonwealth
University,
Richmond   23298

Virginia Polytechnic Institute
and State University,
Blacksburg   24061

Virginia State University,
Petersburg   23803

Virginia Union University,
Richmond   23220

Virginia Wesleyan College,
Norfolk   23502

WASHINGTON
Clark College,
Vancouver   98663

Columbia Basin College,
Pasco   99301

Eastern Washington University,
Cheney   99004

Evergreen State College,
Olympia   98505

Gonzaga University,
Spokane   99258

Griffin College,
Seattle   98121

Lower Columbia College,
Longview   98632

Olympic College,
Bremerton   98310

Pacific Lutheran University,
Tacoma   98447

Peninsula College,
Port Angeles   98362

Pierce College,
Tacoma   98498

Seattle Pacific University,
Seattle   98119

Seattle University,
Seattle   98122

Skagit Valley College,
Mount Vernon   98273

University of Puget Sound,
Tacoma   98416

Walla Walla College,
College Place   99324

Wenatchee Valley College,
Wenatchee   98801

Western Washington
University,
Bellingham   98225

Whitman College,
Walla Walla   99362

Whitworth College,
Spokane   99251

WEST VIRGINIA
Alderson-Broaddus College,
Philippi   26416

Bethany College,
Bethany   26032

Bluefield State College,
Bluefield   24701

Davis and Elkins College,
Elkins   26241

University of Charleston,
Charleston   25304

West Virginia University,
Morgantown   26506

Wheeling Jesuit College,
Wheeling   26003

WISCONSIN
Alverno College,
Milwaukee   53215

Beloit College,
Beloit   53511

Carroll College,
Waukesha   53186

Concordia College,
Mequon   53092

Edgewood College,
Madison 53711

Lakeland College,
Sheboygan 53082

Lakeshore Technical College,
Cleveland 53015

Lawrence University,
Appleton 54912

Madison Area Technical
College,
Madison 53704

Marian College of
Fond du Lac,
Fond du Lac 54935

Marquette University,
Milwaukee 53233

Milwaukee School of
Engineering,
Milwaukee 53201

Mount Mary College,
Milwaukee 53222

Mount Senario College,
Ladysmith 54848

Northeast Wisconsin Technical
College,
Green Bay 54307

Northland College,
Ashland 54806

Ripon College,
Ripon 54971

St. Norbert College,
De Pere 54115

University of Wisconsin,
Eau Claire 54701

University of Wisconsin,
La Crosse 54601

University of Wisconsin,
Oshkosh 54901

University of Wisconsin,
Platteville 53818

University of Wisconsin,
River Falls 54022

University of Wisconsin,
Stevens Point 54481

University of Wisconsin,
Stout 54751

University of Wisconsin,
Superior 54880

University of Wisconsin,
Whitewater 53190

Viterbo College,
La Crosse 54601–4797

WYOMING
Casper College,
Casper 82601

Central Wyoming College,
Riverton 82501

INDEX

Printed in the United States
By Bookmasters